THE CONCISE HISTORY OF

WWI

THE CONCISE HISTORY OF
WWI

First published in the UK in 2013

© Demand Media Limited 2013

www.demand-media.co.uk

Printed and bound in China

ISBN 978-1-909217-35-5

Contents

The Causes of War

It was triggered by two shots from an opportunistic assassin's pistol. It erupted into the most widely devastating war the world had ever seen, involving more than seventy million combatants and killing more than sixteen million people.

The Great War was like no other conflict the world had ever seen, or ever will see again. Of those seventy million military personnel, more than nine million never went home. Advances in the technology of war meant weapons were more deadly than ever, and their effects reached far beyond the battlefields. War spread to each corner of the planet as every one of the world's major powers entered the fray. And when the fighting was over, the 'war to end wars' had resulted in the dismantling of four empires and the redrawing of the map of Europe.

The one thing it didn't do was end war. Despite the formation of the League of Nations in a futile attempt to avert further conflicts, festering nationalism provoked by the Great War and the formation of new, deadly ideologies led eventually to the killing fields of the natural sequel: World War II.

To understand these consequences, and to unravel the tangle of ambitions, treaties and alliances that led inexorably to World War I, it's necessary to delve decades back into history. First, though, let us shed some light on the spark that ignited the powder keg: the assassination

Left: *A would-be assassin attached to the Black Hand secret military society fires at Franz Ferdinand, Archduke of the Austro-Hungarian Empire, and his wife Sophie in Sarajevo on 28 June 1914. A further, successful assassination attempt was made later in the day.*

of Archduke Franz Ferdinand, heir to the throne of the Austro-Hungarian Empire, in Sarajevo on 28 June 1914.

The assassin was Gavrilo Princip, a Serbian student who had been supplied with weapons by the Black Hand, a secret nationalist group opposed to the control of Bosnia and Herzegovina by the Empire. Franz Ferdinand had already survived one assassination attempt by colleagues of Princip when his car stopped on its way out of town and the little Serb stepped forward to seize his opportunity, shooting the Archduke and his wife Sophie. He did not know that his actions would set in train a world-changing chain of events.

After the initial shock of the killing, and as the European powers engaged in a frenzy of diplomatic manoeuvring, the Austro-Hungarians took three weeks to decide how they should react. When it came, their decision was drastic: they would take the opportunity to crush the Serbian nationalist movement and stamp their authority on the Balkans. Declaring that Serbia was involved with the Black Hand, the Empire issued an ultimatum containing ten unacceptable demands that were intended to provoke a limited war. Serbia duly agreed to just eight of the demands, and Austria–Hungary declared war on 28 July 1914.

The chain reaction triggered by the Empire's declaration and the cobweb of alliances that had built up between the European powers over the preceding decades started to unwind. Russia was bound by treaty with Serbia to spring to its aid, and it announced a mobilisation of its vast military machine just one day after Austria's declaration. This was, however, a huge process that would take six weeks or more to complete. Germany, too, was bound by treaty to react: it was an ally of Austria–Hungary, and it lost no time in declaring war against Russia on August 1.

France had signed a treaty with Russia, so it found itself at war with Germany and its Austro-Hungarian allies. Germany, meanwhile, proved itself swifter to go to war than Russia, invading the neutral country of Belgium on August 3 as a way of reaching Paris by the shortest possible route. This action brought a reaction from Britain, which was under a moral obligation to defend France under the terms of a treaty, but was also obliged to defend Belgium under an older agreement. Faced with the German invasion, the King of the Belgians, Albert I, appealed to his British allies for aid, and it was swift in coming. A British ultimatum demanding the withdrawal of German troops from Belgium met with no response, and Britain, her colonies and dominions were thus at war with Germany and the Austro-Hungarian Empire.

The chain reaction continued. While United States President Woodrow Wilson declared his country neutral (a policy that would continue until 1917), Japan had a military agreement with Britain, and declared war on Germany on August 23. Austria-Hungary responded by declaring war on Japan two days later. Italy was an ally of both Germany and Austro-Hungary but was able to declare itself neutral until 1915, when it took the side of the Allies against its two former partners.

So it can be seen that what was intended to be a short, limited war waged by an Austro-Hungarian Empire eager to stamp its authority on Serbia could never have been any such thing. The tangled spider's web of alliances reaching from one end of Europe to the other did as much as any assassin's bullet to ensure the argument escalated from a local dispute into a global conflict. To understand how this complex state of

Far Left: *German Chancellor Otto von Bismarck flanked by Nikolay Girs (left), Russian Foreign Minister, and Austria-Hungary Foreign Minister Count Gustav Kálnoky at Skierniewice, Poland on 15 September 1884. The occasion was a meeting of the Three Emperors League.*

THE CAUSES OF WAR

Right: *Kaiser Wilhelm II of Germany with his military commanders Field Marshal Paul von Hindenburg (left) and General Erich Ludendorff in January 1917*

affairs came about, it's necessary to look further back into the history of Europe.

We can start our research by focusing on the ambitions and actions of one man: Otto von Bismarck. This was a man who, as Prime Minister of Prussia and then Chancellor of the German Empire, figured large in European politics from the 1860s until his dismissal by Kaiser Wilhelm II in 1890. It was Bismarck who, by intrigue and warfare, succeeded in creating that Empire out of a loose collection of confederated German states.

His first step, in 1866, was to reduce Austria's influence as the most important of those states by drawing it into a war over disputed territory in the duchy of Holstein. The seven-week war, in which the Prussian military established its dominance, ended in the creation of the North German Federation with the ceding by Austria of Schleswig, Holstein, Hanover, Hesse, Nassau and Frankfurt. Next, Bismarck turned his attention to the south with the aim of uniting all German states under Prussia. This he did by engineering an 1870/71war with France that led to another Prussian victory, the deposition of Napoleon III in a French civil war and the creation of the Third French Republic. To the

THE CONCISE HISTORY OF **WWI**

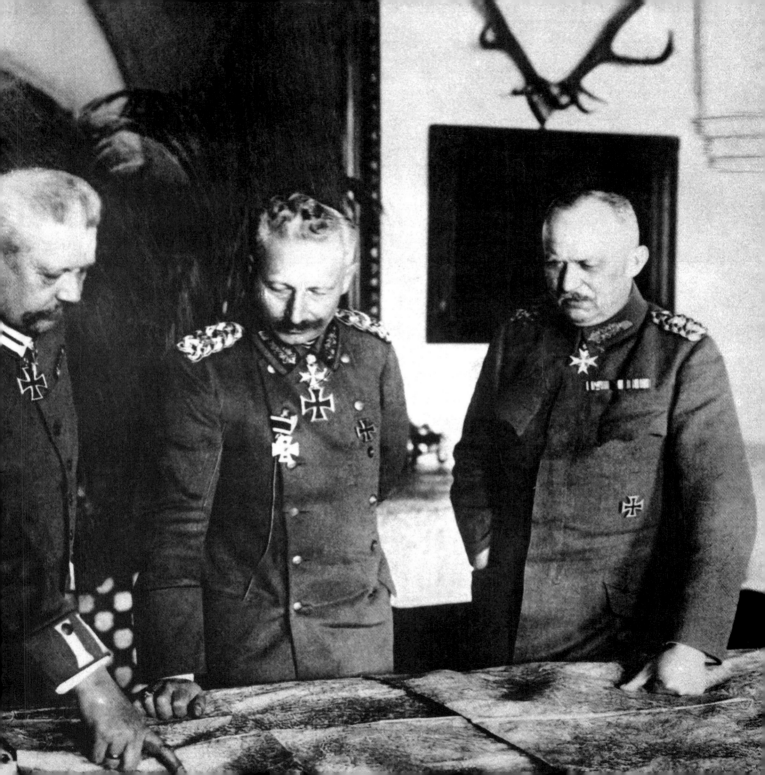

victors went the states of Alsace and Lorraine, and Bismarck was able to create his dreamed-of German Empire when the southern German states agreed to an alliance with their northern counterparts.

Having unified Germany, Bismarck now needed to ensure its stability. This he intended to do by building alliances with key European powers that might conceivably threaten the German Empire. While aware of the danger of French ambitions to retake Alsace and Lorraine, he was not worried by the possibility of a French-British alliance, for Britain was at that time pursuing a policy of non-involvement in European politics. In 1873, Bismarck turned his attention to Russia and the vanquished Austria-Hungary, forming the Three Emperors League, which obliged each of the powers to come to the others' aid in time of war. Russia did not delay long in withdrawing from this pact, however, and in 1879 Bismarck was left with an alliance with Austria-Hungary. It was this treaty that came into play when Russia went to Serbia's aid in 1914.

In 1881, Italy joined the partners to create a Triple Alliance under the terms of which Germany and Austria-Hungary would assist Italy if it was attacked by France. In fact, this alliance proved to be meaningless, for Italy went on, in secret, to negotiate a treaty with the French under which it would remain neutral in the event of a German attack on France – a possibility that became reality in 1914.

But there was more manoeuvring of a highly complex nature to come from Bismarck, who was anxious to ensure that Germany did not become involved in a war on two fronts. In 1887 he concluded a 'reinsurance' treaty with Russia that stated that both powers would remain neutral if either were to become involved in a war with a third party. If that third party were France, Russia would not be obliged to assist Germany; and if Russia found itself at war with Austria-Hungary, Germany would be under no obligation to render assistance to Russia. This treaty lasted no more than three years, for the Russian Tsar Nicholas II allowed it to lapse in 1890, at the same time as Bismarck found his career at an end under the new German Kaiser Wilhelm II.

Two years later, Russia allied itself with France in a move designed to counter the threat of the Triple Alliance of Germany, Austria-Hungary and Italy. Meanwhile, Britain was becoming alert

Far Left: The last German Emperor – Kaiser Wilhelm II of Germany, a grandson of Queen Victoria of Great Britain, ruled from 1888 to 1918

Far Right: *The man whose actions plunged the world into war – Yugoslav nationalist Gavrilo Princip, the assassin of Archduke Franz Ferdinand*

to the emergence of Germany as a major European and colonial power. Wilhelm II's global ambitions were underlined by his country's enormous shipbuilding programme, which was designed to produce a navy to rival Britain's. So Britain signed a military treaty with Japan aimed at frustrating German colonial plans in the Pacific and embarked on its own shipbuilding exercise. By 1906 Britain had launched the massive Dreadnought battleship and was leaving Germany far behind in the naval stakes.

By that time Britain had also strengthened its hand on the diplomatic front, signing an Entente Cordiale with France in 1904 and, three years later, forming a Triple Entente with Russia and France. The Triple Entente was to hold firm until the outbreak of war seven years later. Although it committed all three parties to moral obligations in support of each other, it was actually a treaty Britain had signed in 1839, pledging to defend Belgian neutrality, that was to play a bigger role in forcing Britain into the war.

While the European powers were busy aligning themselves with each other in anticipation of a major conflict, they were also fighting their own wars. Russia found itself embroiled with Japan and suffering a humiliating defeat at the Battle of Tsushima in 1905, when the Japanese annihilated their enemy's entire fleet while losing a mere two torpedo boats. The defeat served to explode the myth of Russian invincibility, contributed to the failed revolution of 1905 and hardened the Tsar's determination to restore his country's status.

There was unrest in other areas, too. War between Italy and Turkey in 1912 resulted in the Turks handing over its possessions of Libya, Rhodes and the Dodecanese Islands to the Italians. Then, having made peace with Italy, Turkey found itself at war over the ownership of Greece, Serbia, Bulgaria and Montenegro. Once again, it was on the losing side and forced to surrender Crete and all of its European possessions. In the Second Balkan war, in 1913, Bulgaria lost out to Romania and gave Adrianople back to Turkey.

Tensions and nationalist feeling were running high in the Balkans. The Slavic peoples of the area, who had endured Ottoman or Austro-Hungarian rule for many years, looked to Russia as their natural ally. Russia, in turn, encouraged this attachment as a means by which it could regain some of its lost prestige.

This was the situation in 1914, when Gavrilo Princip seized his opportunity to kill Franz Ferdinand. The Archduke's Austro-Hungarian Empire was struggling to maintain its grip on the various ethnic groupings in its Balkan possessions; the assassination presented it with a chance to stamp down. Serbia's ally Russia, beset by social unrest, regarded a possible war with Austro-Hungary as a means to quell that turmoil and regain its lost prestige. France was itching for revenge over Germany and for the restoration of Alsace and Lorraine. Germany, like Russia, was experiencing its share of social dissension, and likewise saw war as a cure.

Germany was prepared. It had long expected war with Russia and France, and its military plan, devised by strategist Alfred von Schlieffen, foresaw the obliteration of the French threat inside five weeks, before Russia could mobilise for war on the eastern front. What Germany did not take into account, in the days and weeks following the assassination of Franz Ferdinand, was that Britain would take its obligations to Belgium so seriously and go to war in the little country's defence.

Right: *The funeral of Franz Ferdinand. The bodies of the Archduke and Sophie, Duchess of Hohenberg, were transported from Sarajevo to Vienna by ship and train. Foreign royalty planned to travel to the funeral, but only the immediate imperial family attended*

15

War in Western Europe

1914

It was essential, if Germany's so-called Schlieffen Plan were to succeed, that the threat posed by France should be neutralised before Russia could bring its lumbering military machine into play. Germany was well aware that war on two fronts, in the East and in the West, would stretch its resources to their limits, so speed was of the essence. The aim was to overwhelm France through a lightning-quick attack through neutral Belgian territory and turn southwards in order to encircle the French army on the German border.

In fact it was a modified version of the Schlieffen Plan that was put into action when seven German field armies, under the command of the generals Karl von Bülow and Alexander von Kluck, launched their attack on Belgium on 4 August 1914. The tiny territory of the Duchy of Luxembourg, which had stood in the Germans' way, had been taken two days before, and was allowed to retain its independence throughout the war.

The first setback the German forces encountered came just one day into their attack on Belgium, when the highly fortified city of Liège in the East turned out to be far more resistant than van Bülow had expected. Heavy artillery was brought into play and the city eventually fell on August 16, but by then Germany was facing another threat it had not

anticipated: the entry of Britain into the war. As we have seen, Britain was obliged by treaty to come to the aid of Belgium and the first battle fought by British troops was not long in coming.

Following the fall of Liège, most of the Belgian army fell back to Antwerp and Namur, while their capital city, Brussels, was captured by the advancing Germans on August 20. While the Kaiser's forces avoided Antwerp in the North, they were delayed once more at Namur, between Liège and Brussels, where a siege lasted until August 23.

Meanwhile, the French had their own vision of how the war should play out. Their military strategists had devised Plan XVII, under which the disputed territory of Alsace-Lorraine would be returned to French hands, and five armies were deployed on their borders. The first shots of Plan XVII were heard on August 7, when the French VII Corps launched an attack on Alsace with the

THE CONCISE HISTORY OF **WWI**

aim of taking the cities of Colmar and Mulhouse. Things did not go their way.

On August 14 the First and Second Armies went on the offensive with an assault towards Sarrebourg-Morhange in Lorraine. They suffered heavy losses as the Germans withdrew slowly, in keeping with the Schlieffen Plan, and brought their machine guns into play against infantry troops who were still wearing 19th century uniforms of blue coat and red trousers. The French Third and Fourth Armies advanced towards the River Saar, attacking Briey and Neufchateau, in an attempt to take the city of Sarrebourg, but once again they were beaten back. Mulhouse had been captured, without opposition, by French forces as early as August 7, provoking delirious festivities in France, but German reinforcements were not long in arriving and a counter-attack came two days later. The French commander-in-chief, Marshal Joseph Joffre, despatched a reserve division to help defend the city, but it was too late. Mulhouse fell into German hands once again on August 10, with the French withdrawing towards the town of Belfort.

While Joffre was concerned with executing the French plan for the

Left: *German troops on a battlefield of the Western Front, 1914*

retaking of Alsace-Lorraine, he also had other pressing matters on his mind: the Germans' swift advance through Belgium and their imminent arrival in his own country. The advance came to be called the Rape of Belgium, not only in the sense of the violation of the small, neutral country but also because of war crimes committed by German troops as they swept through. The stories are many and distressing. In towns like Dinant, Tamines, Aarschot and Andenne, hundreds of inhabitants including women and children were executed and their homes burnt by troops apparently in fear of guerrilla attacks. The entire population of Leuven was expelled from the town, inhabitants were shot and the university's priceless library was burnt. Rape as a weapon of terror was widespread and nuns in Brabant were forced to strip by troops who insisted they were spies in disguise.

No doubt some stories were embellished at the time in the cause of propaganda, but it is still no wonder that the British appetite for stemming the Germans' advance was keen. And by the second half of the month of August, that advance had taken the invaders into the North of France. Here they met Joffre's French army and the first six divisions of the British Expeditionary Force (BEF) under the command of Sir John French. The first engagements that ensued came to be known as the Battle of the Frontiers.

This was the situation on 20 August 1914: the French Fifth Army under General Charles Lanrezac was beginning to occupy a 40-kilometre front along the Sambre river, with the Belgian city of Charleroi at its centre and the fortified Naumur at its eastern extremity. To the west were the Cavalry Corps of General André Sordet and the Fifth Army of the BEF at Mons. Lanrezac was faced by 38 German divisions from von Bülow's Second Army and the Third Army.

Joffre ordered Lanrezac to attack despite the latter's weakened state owing to the transfer of troops to Lorraine. In any event, before Lanrezac could launch an assault, on August 21 he found himself under attack from von Bülow in what came to be known as the Battle of Charleroi. Attacks across the river led to the establishment of two bridgeheads that the French, without artillery, were powerless to dislodge. A further attack ensued the following day and on August 23 the French around Charleroi began

Above: *A howitzer is readied for action on the Western Front*

to fall back.

To the east, the German Third Army had crossed the Meuse river but its advance had been stopped by the forces of General Louis Franchet d'Espèrey, who then counter-attacked with success. But Lanrezac was forced to order a withdrawal when Naumur was evacuated and news of the Fourth Army's retreat from the Ardennes came through.

By this time, Kaiser Wilhelm had, according to rumours circulating at the time, scorned the capabilities of the BEF and had ordered his armies to exterminate the 'treacherous' English and 'walk over General French's contemptible little army'. It is not known whether this order was ever truly made or whether it was an invention of the British propaganda machine, but in years to come those regular soldiers who survived the Great War would call themselves the 'Old Contemptibles'.

The BEF found trouble to the west of Lanrezac's retreat three days after the Kaiser's supposed pronouncement, when it encountered a cavalry screen of von Kluck's First Army south-west of Brussels. Field-Marshal French, believing his men were face to face with an inferior German force, ordered an attack. The truth was that French's strength of 80,000 men, in one cavalry and four infantry divisions, was faced by double that number of German troops, although the British had been reinforced by the arrival of French forces along the Mons-Condé Canal the night before.

On August 23 von Kluck launched the Battle of Mons with an assault on the British II Corps led by General Horace Smith-Dorrien. Attacking over open ground, the Germans found themselves vulnerable to the rifle fire of the outnumbered British defenders, who inflicted heavy casualties. The advance was held up until the evening, when the real strength of the enemy became apparent to Smith-Dorrien. As Sordet's cavalry retreated, leaving the right flank exposed, the British in turn fell back to a second defensive line. Von Kluck made no immediate attempt to pursue them. The German advance had been held up for a day.

Back at home, in the years that followed the Battle of Mons, accounts began to circulate of the miraculous appearance of a host of angels, or in some versions phantom archers from the fifteenth century Battle of Agincourt, aiding the British cause on the battlefield. Inspired by a short story written by the Welsh author Arthur Machen (who vehemently denied the veracity of his work of fiction), the legend of the Angels of Mons grew until it gained a sort of acceptance. Needless to say, no concrete evidence of an angelic intervention has ever been found.

In northern France, the German advance continued as the British and French retreated. At the Battle of Le Cateau on August 26, German troops were met by heavy artillery fire from Smith-Dorrien's men but pressed forward again and again until, with cover from Sordet's cavalry, the British withdrew to St Quentin. Of the 40,000 British troops who fought at Le Cateau,

7,812 were killed, wounded or taken prisoner, and 38 artillery pieces were left behind. Despite the dreadful losses, Le Cateau has been hailed as one of the British army's most successful holding actions, and Smith-Dorrien was praised in Britain. Nearer the front, however, French criticised his general for standing and fighting.

As the British withdrew, the French Fifth Army under Lanrezac counterattacked, with partial success, the Germans at St Quentin on August 29, before Joffre ordered further withdrawal. French forces were in action again during the Siege of Maubeuge, just nine kilometres from the Belgian border, between August 24 and September 7. The siege, which took place far behind the front line, saw a German artillery bombardment followed by a storming of the fortress complex and the taking of 40,000 French prisoners.

The German commanders were not to know it, but their cherished Schlieffen Plan was about to come to grief. By the end of August, most of the Allied forces had been forced to fall back towards the Marne river, east and south-east of Paris. French and British commanders were in open disagreement over supposed failings on both sides and the British Secretary of State for War, Field Marshal Herbert Kitchener, had been forced to intervene. As the German First and Second Armies approached Paris, their right flank became exposed as they swerved to the south-east, away from Paris, in a bid to swallow the retreating French armies.

This was an opportunity Joffre was quick to seize. He laid plans to attack the Germans along the length of the front with his Sixth Army of 150,000 men and the BEF's force of 70,000 under the command of Sir John French, on the morning of September 6. Von Kluck's First Army began to turn to face the west, the direction of the coming attack, on September 5, and the First Battle of the Marne began a day sooner than Joffre had planned. The German turn created a 50-kilometre gap between the First and Second Armies, which was reported gleefully by the crews of Allied reconnaissance aircraft, and troops from the BEF were despatched to join the French Fifth Army in pouring through the gap. At the same time, the Fifth Army attacked von Bülow's Second Army.

Between September 6 and 8 the Germans were still hopeful of a breakthrough against the French, but

Above: *An officer rides through the desolation of the battlefield near Amiens*

the latter's Sixth Army received succour with the arrival of 10,000 reserve infantry troops ferried from Paris – some of them in taxis provided by the military governor of the capital. A surprise attack by the Fifth Army of Franchet d'Espèrey against the Second Army on September 8 widened the gap between the German's two armies. It was a rapid success for Franchet d'Espèrey, who had succeeded Lanrezac, sacked for his lack of attacking spirit.

By September 9 it was looking as if the German armies would be encircled and destroyed. The situation appeared so severe to the commanding officer, Chief of Staff Helmuth von Moltke, that he suffered a nervous breakdown and was replaced by his officers. The latter ordered a general retreat to the River

Right: *A French air torpedo is fired from the trenches*

Aisne, where they hoped to regroup. The Schlieffen Plan lay in tatters.

Pursued by the Allies, the German armies withdrew 64 kilometres to a point north of the Aisne, where they dug in. The trenches were to remain for years as stalemate set in. The aftermath of the First Battle of the Marne set the pattern for the Western Front for much of the rest of the war: static fronts on both sides, with retreats and advances, if any, often measured in metres rather than kilometres.

Now began the so-called Race for the Sea, in which each of the opposing forces attempted to outflank the other, with trench systems being extended and inconclusive battles being fought, until by November 1914 the lines reached from the North Sea at Nieuwpoort, Belgium in the North to the French-Swiss border in the South. Along the way many battles were fought as outflanking manoeuvres were tried and failed – the First Battle of the Aisne, the First Battle of Picardy and the Battle of the Yser were among them – and in the end Belgium and France were scarred by 320 kilometres of fortified trenches. France was seriously hampered, too, by the fact that Germany was now occupying territory that accounted for nearly two-thirds of its pig iron production, a quarter of its steel manufacturing and nearly half of its coalmining capacity.

But this was only established after the final German attempt to break through in the Race for the Sea, in the First Battle of Ypres, was repelled. This was one of the most significant battles of the Great War, and not only for the fact that it settled the positions of the opposing forces on the Western Front for years to come. After a series of offensives and counter-offensives, the last great German assault came in mid-October, but it was called off too early, allowing the Allies off the hook. Nevertheless, enormous numbers of casualties were suffered on both sides – up to 85,000 French killed, wounded or missing; over 21,000 Belgians; perhaps as many as 127,000 British; and more than 134,000 Germans – and the result was the end of the British regular army. They were replaced by reserves and, eventually, the masses of a newly conscripted army. While Allied victory, of a kind, was the result of the First Battle of Ypres, no progress had been made and mobile warfare would not be seen again until 1918.

By the spring of 1915 on the Allied

side of the line, Belgian forces controlled a 35-kilometre front along the Yser river and the Yperlee canal, from Nieuwpoort to Boesinghe. The British Expeditionary Force guarded a line stretching to south of St Eloi in the valley of the River Somme. The rest of the line, all the way to the border with Switzerland, was the domain of the French army.

1915

Once the battle lines of the Western Front had been drawn, the two sides searched for ways to break them. As Marshal Joffre's planners pored over the maps, one obvious possibility jumped out at them: a bulge in the line of trenches near the town of Compiègne, on the river Oise. According to Joffre's plan, British and French forces would attack from both sides and cut off the bulge, or salient.

Accordingly, the morning of 10 March 1915 saw an assault by four British divisions (including a large contingent from India) along a three-kilometre front at the village of Neuve Chapelle in the Artois region, following a 35-minute artillery bombardment and supported by aerial attacks by the Royal Flying Corps (RFC). The attack was initially successful, with the defences over-run and the village secured, but the advance was held up by a determined German rearguard and poor communications. Two days later came a counter-attack from forces commanded by Crown Prince Rupprecht and the campaign was called off on March 13. In recapturing just two kilometres of ground, the 40,000 Allied troops who took part in the Battle of Neuve Chapelle had suffered 11,200 casualties – 7,000 British and 4,200 Indian. The Germans had suffered much the same fate.

Elsewhere on the Western Front, German commanders were looking with interest at the Flemish town of Ypres in western Belgium, which had been defended by the British the previous November. The Second Battle of Ypres was to become notorious for a sinister reason: it would see the first large-scale use of gas as a weapon of war on the Western Front, the Germans having already put it to use against the Russians in Poland. Another 'first' came out of Ypres: it was the first time a force from a British colony, the First Canadian Division, defeated a European power on the soil of the old continent.

Ypres consisted, in fact, of six major engagements, lasting from April 22 until May 25: the Battles of Gravenstafel, Saint Julien, Frezenberg and Hooge and two battles of Bellewaarde. Eight infantry divisions were employed on the Allies' side; seven by the Germans. When the fighting ceased, the Allies had suffered 70,000 casualties, Germany half that number.

Germany began its efforts to take the town of Ypres with a two-day bombardment and then released 168 tons of chlorine gas over a 6.5 kilometre front held by French, Moroccan and Algerian troops. German troops had hauled nearly

THE CONCISE HISTORY OF **WWI**

6,000 gas cylinders, each weighing 41 kilograms, to the front by hand and had then opened them one by one, relying on the wind to carry the gas to its target. Needless to say, the wind played tricks and many Germans were killed or incapacitated by their own weapon. On the French side, the number of casualties was terrible: around 6,000 troops died within 10 minutes from asphyxiation or lung damage, and many more were blinded. The heavy gas filling the trenches also forced their inhabitants out to where they were easy prey for German guns. One soldier described the effects of gas as 'drowning on dry land'. He continued: 'The effects are these – a splitting headache and terrific thirst (to drink water is instant death), a knife edge of pain in the lungs and the coughing up of a greenish froth off the stomach and the lungs, ending finally in insensibility and death. The colour of the skin from white turns a greenish black and yellow, the colour protrudes and the eyes assume a glassy stare. It is a fiendish death to die.'

The panic and abandonment of positions that ensued from the gas attack opened up a six-kilometre gap in the front line – a gap the German commanders were not ready to exploit.

The attempts they did make to pour through the gap were met by determined defence on the part of Canadian troops, who improvised gas masks by urinating on cloths and holding them to their faces. Gas was used again in the battle for Ypres, but the Germans made no great advances. By May 25, the Ypres salient had been reduced so that the town was closer to the line. Eventually, it would be so damaged by shelling that hardly a building stood. By July 1915, Allied troops had been supplied with gas masks and anti-asphyxiation respirators.

French troops were in action again in the spring of 1915 when they attempted to take Vimy Ridge, eight kilometres north-east of Arras. The 145-metre ridge was a vital observation point for the Germans and allowed them to protect coalmines in the Lens area. The French 10th Army, after a six-day bombardment, attacked on May 10 and managed to advance five kilometres, but their progress was soon halted. Fighting continued until June 18, but Vimy Ridge was to play a further role later in the war.

While France, Britain and their colonial partners were engaged in the hell that was the Gallipoli peninsula, hundreds of kilometres to the east, in the summer

Far Left: French front-line troops use a periscope to scan enemy positions in 1915

Far Right: *British Royal Aircraft Factory SE-5 fighter aircraft engage in aerial combat with German Fokker D VIIs*

of 1915, stalemate was the situation in the West. Allied reconnaissance efforts, using poorly armed spotter aircraft, were being thwarted by Germany's use of fighter monoplanes, and the 'Fokker Scourge' was to last until the early months of 1916. But in September 1915, as the French mounted an attack in Champagne, the British were also in action in the Battle of Loos.

The assault, commanded by Field Marshal Douglas Haig despite his misgivings about the timing of the venture, was preceded by four days of artillery bombardment during which a quarter of a million shells were fired. Six divisions were committed to the attack on September 25, giving Britain a massive supremacy in numbers over their German enemies: in some places the British had seven men to Germany's one. They had another advantage, too: German gas mask design was deemed too primitive to cope with the 140 tons of chlorine gas the British were to use against them. As had been the case at Ypres, however, the prevailing winds ensured that the gas affected some of those who were using it. Although only seven British troops died, there were more than 2,500 casualties.

To the southern end of the attack, Haig's forces met with success on the first day, taking the town of Loos (which was eventually completely destroyed) and progressing towards the city of Lens. Problems with supplies and the need for reserves brought that day's advance to a halt. Elsewhere, the British gas attack was less effective, even though two divisions managed to gain a foothold on the Hohenzollern Redoubt. The following day the Germans counter-attacked in numbers, having brought up some reserves, and the British, with no preliminary artillery attack to support them, found themselves walking into withering machine gun fire without covering fire. After a few days of on-off engagements, Haig's troops were ordered to retreat on September 28.

A further attack on October 13 was called off when heavy losses and poor weather made defeat inevitable. The number of casualties made sorry reading: 50,000 on the British side, perhaps half that number of Germans. Loos was a failure, but it contributed to Haig's replacement of Sir John French as British Commander-in-Chief later in 1915. Haig's doubts had sealed his reputation as the man for the job.

1916

By the time 1916 dawned, Germany was working to a new plan. The Chief-of-Staff, Erich von Falkenhayn, insisted in a Christmas Day letter to the Kaiser that the way to victory in the war lay not in the East, against Russia, but in the West, against France. In order to starve Britain and remove it from the war, he argued, a policy of unrestricted submarine warfare (which ran the risk of committing the United States to the war) should be conducted against merchant shipping. At the same time, a major set-piece victory against the French would bring Britain to the negotiating table or ensure its defeat. The Kaiser was persuaded by von Falkenhayn's reasoning, and thus set in train the events that led to the Battle of Verdun. It was a battle that would eventually cost von Falkenhayn his job.

Verdun held a special, symbolic place in the hearts of the French people, as it does today. A fortress since Roman times, it had been the last fortification to fall to the enemy in the Franco-Prussian war of 1870-71 and had been further strengthened since that time.

The German Chief-of-Staff, through a terrifying bombardment, planned to 'bleed France white' by drawing troops from an enormous area to the defence of the fortress town. In his favour was the fact that Verdun formed a salient into German lines, allowing it to be attacked on three sides.

Postponed from its original proposed start date of February 12 to the 21st of that month, the assault was to be preceded by a 21-hour bombardment. Marshal Joffre, apprised of the imminent attack, duly rushed reinforcements to the French Second Army, while the fortress commander, Lieutenant-Colonel Emile Driant, attempted to strengthen Verdun's defences. His 200,000 defenders, on the east bank of the Meuse river, faced a formidable foe: a million German troops of the German Fifth Army under Crown Prince Wilhelm.

The Prince's opening gambit – 100,000 shells fired every hour from 1,400 guns along a 13-kilometre front – was intended to wipe out the French defence before the infantry started their advance. It failed. Miraculously, half of the defenders remained in place, so Wilhelm renewed the bombardment but by the end of the first day the Germans

OLD HUN LINE.

had succeeded only in taking the French front-line trenches. On the second day the next line of trenches was over-run and the defenders were forced back to within eight kilometres of Verdun itself, although outlying forts were still holding out and more reinforcements were on their way.

As one of those forts fell, Joffre reminded his commanders that any

Above: *Grinning victors in a captured German trench, Battle of the Somme, 1916*

Right: *A German casualty of the Battle of Flers-Courcelette, part of the Somme Offensive of 1916*

man who ceded ground to the Germans would be court-martialled; to surrender Verdun was unthinkable. In place of a general who had fallen out of favour he appointed Philippe Pétain – later to achieve notoriety as the Chief of State of Vichy France during World War II – to command the defence. 'Ils ne passeront pas!' Pétain assured Joffre. 'They shall not pass!'

It was a significant appointment. Pétain, determined to inflict as many casualties on the German as possible while conceding the inevitability of enormous French losses, reorganised the use of artillery and ensured an effective supply route remained open. The next German offensive, on March 6, met with stern resistance as French reinforcements continued to arrive: of the 330 infantry regiments the French army possessed, 259 saw service at Verdun. On April 9 the third major German offensive started, again Pétain's defences held and again attacks were met by counter-attacks.

As the weeks wore on Pétain was promoted, to be replaced by General Robert Nivelle, and the Germans started to use a deadly new chemical: phosgene gas. Still the victory they craved refused to come their way, and they had other worries: the British were starting a major offensive in the Somme, brought forward from its intended date as a means of diverting German manpower away from Verdun. In addition, a Russian offensive in the East was a further drain on resources.

The weeks turned into months, the French started to retake ground captured by the Germans and gradually the latter began to realise that von Frankenhayn's plan to bleed France white was never going to succeed. The Battle of Verdun dragged on until December 1918, having lasted nearly ten months and cost both sides unimaginable numbers of lives: of 542,000 French casualties, 362,000 were killed; German losses were estimated at 434,000, of which 336,000 died. And neither side had gained any advantage.

The offensive that led to the Battle of the Somme had been planned as far back as late 1915, and it had been intended at that point as a joint French-British operation. Joffre had wanted the battle to drain the German army of reserves while resulting in territorial gains, much as his opponents had viewed the Battle of Verdun. In the end, it was Verdun that led to the Somme offensive being brought forward a month to 1 July 1916.

That date will be inscribed in the annals of warfare for all time. The first day of the offensive, launched on a 30-kilometre front north of the Somme river between Arras and Albert, accounted for 58,000 British troops, a third of them killed. That figure remains a grim record for one day of war.

The assault had been preceded, as was the norm, by an artillery bombardment of the German lines that began on June 24 and continued for eight days. Three thousand guns – half British, half French – dealt the heavy blows that were supposed to obliterate the forward German defences, enabling British troops to saunter across No Man's Land meeting little resistance. The infantry were to be aided by a creeping barrage of artillery fire, aimed just ahead of the advancing troops and moving forward as the men advanced. Field Marshal Haig ordered General Sir Henry Rawlinson, whose Fourth Army would spearhead the assault, to consolidate after a limited advance, while to the north other forces would attempt a complete breakthrough of the German defences. Haig, a cavalry man, was convinced that horse-borne forces would be able to deliver the coup de grâce once the German lines had been

breached, and then the way would be open to advance to the towns of Cambrai and Douai. The numerical odds were stacked in favour of the attacking British, who called on 27 divisions consisting of 750,000 men while the German defenders would have 16 divisions of the Second Army on hand.

What Haig's planning failed to take into account was that the artillery's shells would prove unequal to the task of destroying the enemy's front-line barbed wire or robustly built concrete bunkers. Many shells failed to explode, and the German troops simply took shelter in the safety of their bunkers until the bombardment stopped, emerging to man their machine guns.

The assault on July 1 was announced with the detonation of an 18,000-kilogram mine that had been laid, after seven months of tunnelling by Royal Engineers, beneath German front lines on Hawthorn Ridge Redoubt. That massive explosion was followed ten minutes later, at 0730 hours, by the detonation of 16 further mines and the first wave of troops going over the top. Not surprisingly, given the amount of warning the Germans had been given by the bombardment and the failure of the artillery to break the defences, those troops met with little success, on July 1 or on any other day.

They met, instead, deadly machine gun fire that killed them, wounded them or forced them back into their trenches. Many soldiers, weighed down by heavy supplies and expecting an easy passage to the German lines, took no more than a few steps before they were struck down by defenders who were presented with sitting targets. Further south, French forces, whose offensive had been preceded by a much smaller bombardment, were more successful, but even they could do little more than consolidate their small gains rather than exploit them.

Nevertheless, despite appalling losses, Haig persisted with his approach, believing as the battle raged on that the Germans would eventually succumb to exhaustion and that victory was imminent. Small advances were sometimes made, but they were short-lived and never followed up. German commanders took the opportunity to transfer troops from Verdun, doubling the number of defenders, and reorganise the lines.

The British made use of tanks for the first time in the Battle of Flers-Courcelette on September 15, which saw 15 divisions deployed and gained less than a kilometre of ground. The original number of 50 tanks had been reduced to 24 by mechanical and other failures and, while they had the desired shock effect on German troops, proved unreliable and difficult to control. Some even fired on their own infantry.

The battles continued throughout October, at Morval, Thiepval Ridge, Transloy, Ancre Heights and Chaulnes among other locations and, as French forces started to gain ground at Verdun, Joffre urged Haig to carry on. It was essential, he reasoned, that the British should continue to occupy the Germans while his forces carried on their good work at Verdun. So it went on until, on November 13, Britain launched what would turn out to be its final effort of the Battle of the Somme: the Battle of Ancre, which resulted in the capture of the field fortress of Beaumont Hamel.

On November 18, hampered by snow, the Somme offensive ground to a halt. It had gained the British and French allies 12 kilometres of ground and cost around 420,000 British and 200,000 French casualties. On the German side,

losses were estimated at half a million.

If there was one positive aspect of the Somme, it was the British re-evaluation of the usefulness of smaller tactical units of infantry troops. Beforehand, commanders had argued that a company of 120 men was the smallest effective unit possible; afterwards, they often followed the example of the French and Germans in opting for platoons of 10 or so men.

Germany had been making changes, too. In August 1916, after the failure at Verdun, Erich von Falkenhayn had resigned as Chief-of-Staff, to be replaced

at the head of the war effort by General Paul von Hindenburg and General Erich Ludendorff. With their offensive capabilities severely depleted by Verdun and the Somme, they decided to switch their strategy to one of defence in the West while concentrating their offensive effort elsewhere. Von Hindenburg and Ludendorff opted to erect a defensive position behind a section of the front, to be called the Hindenburg Line and intended to shorten the German front by about 50 kilometres, thus freeing 10 divisions for other purposes. The line of fortifications, first spotted by British aircraft in November 1916, ran from Arras south to St Quentin, between five and 50 kilometres behind the front line.

1917

The Germans' withdrawal behind the Hindenburg Line started in February 1917 and was completed on April 5. The Allied forces found they had left behind a vast desolate territory, the result of the German's 'scorched earth' policy – the removal of any resource that might be of use to the enemy.

While the German troops were withdrawing behind the line, highly

Left: *Wounded at the Battle of Menin Road, 1917*

Far Left: *Field Marshal Paul von Hindenburg, after whom the Hindenburg Line was named*

significant moves were being made in the waters of the Atlantic Ocean. Germany had been wise enough, following the 1915 sinking of the British liner *Lusitania* with the loss of 1,195 lives, to bring to an end its policy of unrestricted submarine warfare for fear of an American entry into the war, but its hand was being forced by food shortages. Emboldened by the belief that Britain could be starved

out of the war and that it would take the US many months to become an effective force on the Western Front, Germany resumed it attacks on merchant shipping in February 1917. A little over a month later, on April 6, the US declared war on Germany – a declaration that was to have a drastic effect on the outcome of the Western Front conflict.

Three days later came another

THE CONCISE HISTORY OF **WWI**

dramatic event: the sweeping away of firmly entrenched German defenders on the heights of Vimy Ridge, 12 kilometres north-east of Allied-held Arras, by the men of the Canadian Corps. Germany, having gained control of the ridge in September 1914, had wasted no time in building deep, seemingly impregnable defensive positions protected by machine gun emplacements. It then set about the destruction of the town with heavy artillery, seeing off French and British attempts in 1915 and 1916 to gain control of the ridge with massive loss of life on the part of the attackers.

Come the spring of 1917, the Canadian Corps, under the command of British General Julian Byng, were given the task of taking the ridge. Preparations took the form of the digging of miles of tunnels and aerial reconnaissance using observation balloons. At dawn on April 9, following a three-week artillery bombardment, four Canadian divisions attacked, supported by a creeping barrage – and they succeeded where others had failed. In spite of a snowstorm, the Canadian First Division had taken German front-line positions within half an hour, and a further 30 minutes was enough for the second line

WAR IN WESTERN EUROPE

to be captured.

By April 12, with the taking of Hill 145, the highest point, what had at one point seemed an impossible task was complete: Vimy Ridge was under Allied control, and there it was to remain for the rest of the war. Victory had come after the Allies' most successful assault on the Western Front so far. There had been 20,000 German casualties while 3,598 Canadians had been killed and a further 10,000 wounded. The brilliance of the operation was recognised with the award of four Victoria Crosses.

Sadly, its success was not followed up, and meanwhile, Allied aircraft were taking a pounding from their better trained and equipped German counterparts. The Arras assault saw the loss of 316 British and 114 Canadian air crews, against 44 German losses. The RFC dubbed the month Bloody April.

April was the cruellest month elsewhere, too. The Second Battle of the Aisne – the main action of an offensive named after its instigator, Commander-in-Chief Robert Nivelle – was an utter catastrophe for the French. Far from the 48-hour breakthrough that had been planned for the 7,000 guns and 1.2 million troops, it achieved almost nothing in terms of ground won, brought an abrupt end to Nivelle's career and triggered mutiny among the men.

Nivelle, who had replaced Joffre at the head of French forces in December 1916, had rashly assured the government that his tactics would end the war within two days. But politicians and military men expressed their disapproval loudly, and delays and leaks put paid to his plans. By the time the Nivelle Offensive was launched on April 16, the Germans had been familiar with the tactics for some time and had taken defensive measures to counteract them.

After a week of diversionary attacks by British forces in Arras, 19 divisions of the French Fifth and Sixth Armies launched an assault on April 16 along an 80-kilometre front from Soissons to Reims. Ranged against them, on higher ground, was the German Seventh Army, which acquitted itself well. The first day of battle alone resulted in 40,000 French casualties, putting it almost on a par with the British disaster in the Somme a year earlier. The French tanks brought into action fared no better: 150 were lost on the first day. The following day saw the repelling by the German First Army of a further attack by the French Fourth

Above: *German troops launch an assault early in the war*

Army east of Reims.

Both assaults had been hampered by sloping terrain and the incorrect deployment of one of Nivelle's tactics – the creeping barrage – which meant troops were forced to advance without cover. But Nivelle was undeterred by the initial lack of success, and carried on attacking in full strength until April 20. Thereafter the offensive was scaled down. Gains made by the French were few and far between, although a four-kilometre length of the Hindenburg Line had been taken by May 5. A final gambit, a four-day assault, proved fruitless and the campaign was called off completely

on May 9. By that time, French casualties had totalled 187,000 while the Germans had lost 168,000.

What's more, morale among the French troops had been shattered. On May 3, men of the French Second Colonial Division, who had already experienced the trauma of Verdun, refused orders, reporting for service drunk and without their weapons. In the absence of severe punishment, mutiny spread and 20,000 men deserted their posts. It was only through appeals to the men's patriotic instincts, alongside the belated instigation of mass arrests and trials, that they agreed to return to

Far Right: *Mortar shells rain down on barbed wire during the Battle of Vimy Ridge, 1917*

the trenches, although they still showed a marked reluctance to take part in offensive action.

The failure of Nivelle's brainchild led to him being sacked and replaced by Pétain, whose military thinking erred on the more cautious side. Pétain managed to quell the disquiet among the troops by improving trench conditions and, more significantly, refraining from offensive operations.

The month of June 1917 saw an upturn in the fortunes of the Allied forces with one of the most successful local operations of the Great War. The Battle of Messines, centred on a ridge south-east of Ypres, was launched by the British Second Army under General Herbert Plumer on June 7. The operation, which saw casualties among defenders exceed those of the attackers for the first time on the Western Front, resulted in a significant boost for morale among the Allies.

The assault was to precede the much larger Third Battle of Ypres, to become known as Passchendaele, and it started with a bang – or rather, 19 bangs. Eighteen months previously, Plumer had ordered the laying of 22 mines underneath German lines the length of

the ridge. His plan was to blow the lot at 0310 on June 7, following up with an infantry and tank assault, a gas attack and an artillery barrage. Eight thousand metres of tunnels were dug as German tunnellers, in turn, sought to thwart the British sappers' efforts – they managed to discover one mine. Occasionally the two sides would meet and engage in subterranean hand-to-hand combat.

Bombardment of the German lines by 2,300 guns and 300 heavy mortars began on May 21 and continued until 20 minutes before zero hour. In the eerie silence that followed, German defenders raced to man their machine guns and send up flares to illuminate British movements. Then 600 tons of explosive sent the crest of the ridge sky high. They say the explosion, the largest devised by man up to that point, was heard by British Prime Minister David Lloyd George in Downing Street, London, and even in Dublin. Around 10,000 German troops perished in the instant of the explosions.

Now came an advance by nine divisions of British infantry, protected by a creeping barrage, tanks and projectors that hurled gas canisters into what was left of the German trenches. Every single

objective was taken in the first three hours of the assault and reserves from the British Fifth Army and French First Army reached their targets by the afternoon. Despite counter-attacks between June 8 and 14, the Allies secured the entirety of the Messines salient. Twenty-five thousand German casualties were recorded, against 17,000 for the Allies.

Two of the mines laid so painstakingly by British sappers remained undetonated. One exploded during a lightning storm in 1955, with the loss of one cow. The other lies, still undetonated, under a Belgian farmer's barn. The farmer is said to be unconcerned.

Another fillip for the Allied forces came in June 1917 in the form of the first arrivals in France of American troops. Although they did not begin to man trenches in divisional strength until October, being in need of training and equipment, the American Expeditionary Force provided a boost for the morale of Allied soldiers wearied by years of constant combat.

Meanwhile, there was the matter of the Third Battle of Ypres to attend to. This was intended to be Field Marshal Douglas Haig's decisive strike, the Allies' breakthrough on the mud of Flanders, but in the end it achieved much less. And what it did achieve came at a shocking cost in human lives. Nowadays, Third Ypres is usually referred to as Passchendaele, after the village that finally fell to the Allies on 6 November 1917, and the tactics employed by Haig over the three months of attrition warfare – trying to wear down the enemy's numbers and effectiveness through sustained attack – have stirred strong emotions ever since.

Haig, who had long planned the battle, was spurred by the failure of the French Nivelle Offensive to launch his attack in the late summer. He aimed to reach and destroy the German submarine bases on the Belgian coast that had wrought such destruction on the oceans that Admiral Sir John Jellicoe had warned that continued similar losses of shipping would stop Britain waging war into 1918. Haig also believed that the German army was close to breaking point – a belief that had sustained him through the Somme offensive of the previous year. He had been proved wrong on that occasion, and he was to be proved wrong again.

There were certainly indicators in favour of a third battle of Ypres: the success of the Messines initiative – Plumer argued that the advantage should be pressed home immediately, although Haig disagreed – and the possibility at the time that Russia might withdraw from the war in the East, leaving Germany free to redeploy forces to the Western Front.

So on July 18 an immense artillery bombardment began. It involved 3,000 guns firing 4.25 million shells and gave the German Fourth Army more than adequate warning that a major offensive

Far Right:
*Group Captain
Lionel Rees,
commanding
officer of 32
Squadron of
the Royal Flying
Corps, awarded
the Victoria Cross
with this citation:
'Major Rees, whilst
on flying duties,
sighted what he
thought was a
bombing party
of our machines
returning home,
but were in fact
enemy aircraft.
Major Rees was
attacked by one
of them, but after
a short encounter
it disappeared,
damaged. The
others then
attacked him at
long range, but
he dispersed
them, seriously
damaging two
of the machines.
He chased two
others but was
wounded in the
thigh, temporarily
losing control of
his aircraft. He
righted it and
closed with the
enemy, using up
all his ammunition,
firing at very close
range'*

was about to be launched. On the last day of July the British Fifth Army, led by Sir Hubert Gough, with 1 Corps of Plumer's Second Army to the right and a corps of the French First Army to the left – 12 divisions in total – initiated the assault across an 18-kilometre front. The Germans were well placed to repel the British advance across the Menin Road, limit them to small gains around Pilckem Ridge and hold off the French further north.

Then came the rain. The lowlands of Flanders were turned into a glutinous, almost impassable swamp by the heaviest rains for 30 years, exacerbated by the damage on the land wrought by the British artillery barrage. Tanks, stuck fast in the quagmire, were rendered useless and infantry troops struggled to move forward. Mud had almost become their worst enemy, and no progress could be made until August 16, when the British made small gains while sustaining heavy casualties in the four-day Battle of Langemarck.

Haig reassessed his resources and moved Gough's forces further north, replacing them with those of Plumer. The latter favoured a sequence of small achievements over large breakthroughs, and a series of gains was to follow. From September 20 the cumulative result of the Battles of Menin Road Bridge, Polygon Wood and Broodseinde was British possession of the ridge east of Ypres.

Haig was now more convinced than ever that the German army was close to collapse, and determined to continue the attack towards Passchendaele Ridge 10 kilometres from Ypres. The October Battle of Poelcappelle and the First Battle of Passchendaele achieved little of note, and the British were by now facing increasing numbers of German reserves who had been released from the Eastern Front. In addition, the Germans were now using the more effective mustard gas rather than chlorine gas or phosgene. Still Haig, displaying the inflexibility for which he is heavily criticised to this day, pressed on. He would not – perhaps could not – call off the slaughter until the village of Passchendaele was captured by British and Canadian forces on November 6.

The number of casualties suffered in Third Ypres, in return for the widening of the salient by a few kilometres, are disputed. Some sources put the Allies losses as high as 448,000, and those of

Germany at 410,000, while others opt for 200,000 and 217,000 respectively. Whatever the true numbers, it is arguable they could have been much lower if Haig had been willing to unbend and call an earlier end to the offensive. Passchendaele has been called 'the greatest martyrdom of the war' and has become a byword for futile slaughter.

Still, little time was lost before British forces were in action in a major offensive again, this time at the Battle of Cambrai. This battle marked the first time massed tanks had been used on a battlefield, and this time they were not bogged down by mud. Lieutenant-Colonel John Fuller of the Tank Corps was insistent that the tank would come into its own on drier ground between the Canal du Nord and the St Quentin Canal, and he was supported in this view by Field Marshal Julian Byng, commander of the Third Army. Haig was at first unconvinced but eventually conceded the argument and gave Byng the go-ahead for a major offensive, despite the fact that worsening weather threatened to diminish the effectiveness of the mass tank assault.

On the morning of November 20, 476 tanks accompanied by six

infantry and two cavalry divisions and 1,000 guns, advanced across a 10-kilometre front. This time there was no preliminary artillery bombardment, which ensured the element of surprise was intact, and this time 14 squadrons of the RFC were standing by to lend support. Within hours the German Second Army had been forced back six kilometres to Cambrai and the three trench systems of the Hindenburg Line had been breached for the first time. Eight thousand prisoners and 100 guns had been taken.

Both sides were somewhat taken aback by the speedy gains of the first day. Haig authorised a continuation but the British were hampered by a lack of support, and progress faltered. German forces launched counter-attack after counter-attack using infantry infiltration tactics to penetrate enemy lines and, after a week of battle, had regained almost all of the ground they had lost.

Tanks had been proved to be an effective weapon in some situations – even where trenches had to be overcome – but the Allies lost around 45,000 men in the Battle of Cambrai and gained no ground. German casualties numbered around 50,000.

1918

The arrival of American troops on European soil had changed the rules of the game. The two men at the head of the German war machine, General Erich Ludendorff and Field Marshall Paul von Hindenburg, were agreed that the only route to German victory now open to them lay in a major decisive assault along the Western Front before the strength of the Americans became decisive. With the signing of the Treaty of Brest-Litovsk on 3 March 1918, Russia withdrew from the war, freeing 33 divisions for duties in the West. The omens were good for Germany: it had 192 divisions available, compared to the Allies' 178; the armies of France, Britain and its Empire were sorely depleted, and were suffering from a lack of unified command and lowered morale; and the Americans had not yet been fully readied for war. It was in this context that Ludendorff planned a massive offensive aimed at separating the British from the French and driving them back to the Channel ports. The first steps were taken in the Third Battle of Aisne, from 27 May to 6 June 1918.

Ludendorff determined to reclaim

the Chemin des Dames Ridge, which had been lost during the French Nivelle Offensive of April 1917, with a massed attack relying on surprise. The ridge was held by four divisions of the British IX Corps, who had been sent there from Flanders to recuperate; some recuperation! The troops were led by General Denis Duchêne with Lieutenant-General Sir Alexander Hamilton Gordon his second in command. When the German attack came, Hamilton Gordon tried to save his fatigued troops by recommending a policy of defence in depth, but Duchêne insisted on sending them to the front line.

The assault came on May 27, begun by an artillery bombardment from 4,000 guns along a 40-kilometre front together with a gas attack. Hamilton Gordon's IX Corps was virtually wiped out in the opening barrage. Then came an advance by 17 divisions of infantry commanded by Crown Prince Wilhelm and making rapid progress through the gap. They reached the Aisne in less than six hours, having broken through eight more Allied divisions, and by the end of the first day they had arrived at the River Vesle. After three days the Germans had taken 50,000 prisoners and 800 guns, and by June 3

Left: *German prisoners taken during an American assault during the Battle of St-Mihiel, 1918*

Right: *British casualties of a gas attack during the Fourth Battle of Ypres, 1918*

they were within 90 kilometres of Paris.

Familiar problems dogged Wilhelm's men, however. There were shortages of supplies and reserves, the troops were fatigued and there was the constant threat of Allied counter-attacks. By June 6 the advance had halted, but there was a crisis in the Allied ranks. Duchêne, the object of Pétain's disdain, was dismissed and Pétain found himself being made subservient to a new Allied Supreme Commander: Marshal Ferdinand Foch. The Allies had sought to solve their problems of command by appointing one man to oversee all operations.

Meanwhile, American forces had played their first sustained role in the war during the German Aisne Offensive. On May 28, a regiment of the American First Division had captured the village of Cantigny, the site of a fortified German observation post. Aided by French aircraft, artillery and flamethrower teams, the Americans followed 12 French tanks into the village and expanded their front by around two kilometres. Seven German counter-attacks followed, but the US forces held their ground and took 100 prisoners while suffering 1,000 casualties. Victory at Cantigny was followed by further successes.

By the summer of 1918, 300,000 American soldiers were arriving every month, and by the end of the war 2.1 million US troops had seen service on the Western Front. The vast numbers of fresh combatants served to counter the swelling legions of redeployed German troops and had a decisive effect on the eventual outcome of the struggle.

Two related battles – at Château-Thierry on June 3 and 4 and at Belleau Wood from June 6 to 26 – saw the American Expeditionary Force in prolonged action. They resulted in the capture of a wood on the road between Metz and Paris that had been taken by the German Seventh Army as part of the Aisne Offensive. In the first action, the

US Second and Third Divisions headed by Commander-in-Chief John J 'Black Jack' Pershing, together with men of the French Tenth Colonial Division, pushed the Germans back across the Marne to Jaulgonne.

Two days later, the Second Division's Marine Corps suffered terrible casualties in crossing an open wheat field in the face of sweeping machine gun fire while taking Belleau Wood. Back came the Germans to retake the prized wood, and back once again came the Americans. By June 26 the US forces, who suffered nearly 10,000 casualties, had been forced to capture the wood no fewer than six times to eject the Germans decisively. Château-Thierry/ Belleau Wood was hailed as a major turning point in the war.

Things were turning against Germany, and not just on the battlefield. The influenza pandemic of 1918, which infected 500 million people worldwide and killed between 50 and 100 million of them — between three and five per cent of the world's population — hit the Central Powers of Germany and Austria particularly hard, and hit them before the Allied countries. The virus spread rapidly in the confined environment of the trenches, and it could not have come at a

THE CONCISE HISTORY OF **WWI**

worse time for the Kaiser's men. Morale among the German troops was drooping after the series of Allied successes, and it took a further battering from the bug.

Against this backdrop, Australian and American forces launched the Battle of Le Hamel on July 4 with a view to capturing a small town and its surrounding woods around 25 kilometres to the east of Amiens, in the Somme. The attack was intended to avert the problem that German fire would pose to subsequent operations led by General Sir Henry Rawlinson's Fourth Army. In command of the Australian Fourth Division was General Sir John Monash, who succeeded in imposing absolute secrecy (avoiding the traditional preliminary bombardment) while drawing up plans for 'peaceful penetration', and made use of massed machine guns, artillery, aircraft and 60 tanks. Monash's plans worked like a dream. The defences were light, the Germans were caught napping and it was all over in 93 minutes, at a cost of 1,000 Australian and American casualties. Some 1,500 prisoners were taken.

It looked as if the tide had turned decisively in favour of the newly reinforced Allies, and the next major engagement served to strengthen that view. The Second Battle of the Marne started out as a large German offensive aimed at striking a war-winning blow but turned into a major Allied victory. When it was over even some German commanders conceded that the war was lost.

Ludendorff, believing Germany's best chances of victory lay in Flanders, prepared a large diversionary attack designed to lure Allied forces from Belgium to the Marne. While huge numbers of Allied troops were engaged there, he reasoned, Germany could launch a massive offensive further north. The Marne operation was to be set in train on the back of an earlier push towards Paris that had recaptured the Chemin des Dames ridge, which had been lost to the French in 1917.

On July 15, 23 divisions of Germany's First and Third Armies attacked the French Fourth Army, commanded by General Henri Gouraud, to the east of Reims. At the same time, to the west, 17 divisions of the Seventh Army aided by the new German Ninth Army launched an assault against the French Sixth Army led by General Jean Degoutte. British, Italian and 85,000 American troops were also available to the French.

Gouraud rallied his troops with

a stirring speech in which he called on them to resist the coming assault. 'The bombardment will be terrible,' he conceded, but: 'You will endure it without weakness. The attack in a cloud of dust and gas will be fierce, but your positions and your armament are formidable. The strong and brave hearts of free men beat in your breasts. None will look behind, none will give way. Every man will have but one thought – "Kill them, kill them in abundance, until they have had enough."'

Gouraud's words were prophetic and Ludendorff's objective of splitting the French forces was soon in doubt; the eastern attack failed in short order and was halted at 11am on the first day. To the east, however, the German offensive broke through the French Sixth Army and crossed the Marne. Six divisions of the Seventh Army established a vast bridgehead before the French Ninth Army, assisted by British, American and Italian forces, put a stop to the advance on July 17.

The time was ripe for Foch, in his new role as Allied Supreme Commander, to initiate a counter-attack, and this he did on July 18, committing 24 French divisions plus American, British and Italian troops and 350 tanks to the task. His objective of eliminating a large German salient among the French lines was achieved, with the French Tenth and Sixth Armies advancing five miles on the first day and the Ninth Army making progress to the west. In response, the Germans ordered a retreat and by August 3 they were back where they had been before their spring 1918 offensive: at the Aisne-Vesle rivers. By August 6 the Allied counter-attack was called to a halt with the Germans now entrenched. When the fighting finished and the casualties were counted, it emerged that Germany had suffered 168,000, with France incurring 95,000 losses, Britain 13,000 and the US 12,000.

Ludendorff's plans for Flanders were in ruins and Germany was to make no further big attempts to win the war. Two days after the cessation of the Second Battle of the Marne, the Allies launched another major assault that was to become known as the Hundred Days Offensive and would lead to the end of the Great War.

On the battlefield in the Battle of Amiens were 12 French, five Australian, three British and one American division, assisted by more than 1,100 French aircraft, 800 British aircraft and 532

tanks. The Germans could call on 10 active divisions and four reserves, in addition to a mere 365 aircraft. Allied forces advanced the remarkable distance of over seven miles on the first day, with Rawlinson's Fourth Army playing the leading role. Ludendorff was realistic about his men's fortunes, calling the first day of the battle 'the black day of the German army'.

Fighting continued on the days that followed, and by August 12 it was over. German morale had plummeted to new depths while that of the Allies was rising to new heights. The Allies now had 216 divisions at their disposal while the Germans could field only 197. Large numbers of German troops began to surrender as the Hundreds Days Offensive continued with the Second Battle of the Somme (August 21 to September 2), which pushed the

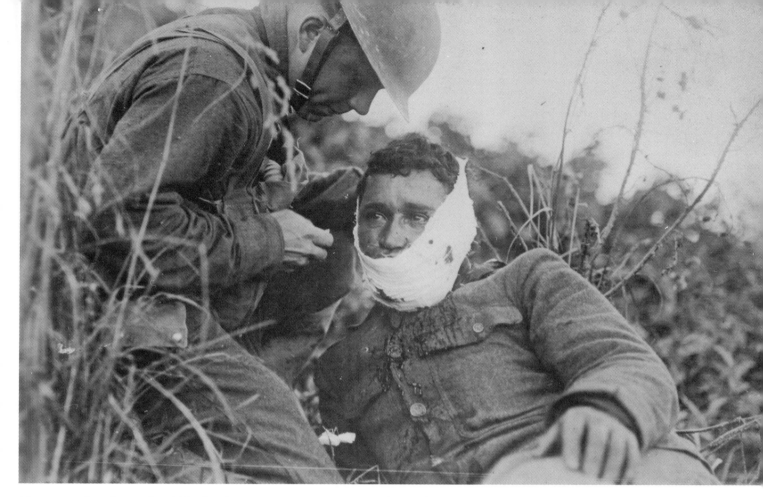

Above: *An American soldier receives medical attention for his wounds, 1918*

Germans back to the Hindenburg Line. Now Marshal Foch launched a series of concentric attacks on the German lines, resulting in battles at St Quentin Canal, Ypres for the fifth and final time, Cambrai once again and many other locations.

At Cambrai the British and Canadians broke through the Hindenburg Line on October 8, and this final straw seemed to persuade the German military commanders that the war had to be brought to an end. Prince Maximilian of Baden was appointed Chancellor of Germany so that he could negotiate an armistice, while Ludendorff, who was opposed to the talks, was forced out of his position and fled to Sweden. Fighting was continuing, but the route to an armistice was clear. Soon, the last bullet fired on the Western Front left its barrel.

Right: *A post-war inspection party tours the ruins of the Belgian town of Ypres in 1919*

THE CONCISE HISTORY OF **WWI**

Life in the Trenches

Any conversation about World War I and its Western Front inevitably at some point diverts to discuss the life of the wretches who manned the trenches day in, day out on both sides of the divide. The Great War has provided history's most prominent example of trench warfare, which has become synonymous with attrition warfare, stalemate and the futility of war.

Whether they answered to the nickname of Tommy or Fritz, whether they were fighting for King or Kaiser, soldiers in the trenches led lives that were nasty, brutish and sometimes tragically short. They faced periods of intense danger and times of brain-numbing boredom. They were required to show superhuman bravery, unswerving loyalty to their cause and unquestioning obedience. They often lived in shockingly squalid conditions among vermin whose sole aim, it seemed, was to make their lives unendurable. Death, appalling injury and destruction surrounded them. Enemies whose only wish was to kill them lurked close by, sometimes as little as 30 metres away. Up to a third of Allied casualties on the Western Front were sustained within the trenches themselves. And if the enemy didn't get you, disease was often not far behind.

To alleviate the misery, the trench-bound soldier might indulge in some

graveyard humour, dream of home and loved ones or revel in the camaraderie that always arises when men are flung together in support of a common cause. He might share a private joke with his mates, at the expense of those who commanded him.

Of course, not all Great War soldiers served in the trenches; far from it. Behind the front line lay a great mass of stores, workshops, headquarters, the supply lines that were vital to keep the war effort going, training centres and so on. In these areas could be found the majority of troops. Behind and to the sides of the infantry in the trenches

THE CONCISE HISTORY OF **WWI**

could also be found the supporting forces of the artillery, the observers, the engineers, the machine gunners and the mortar operators.

Left: *Canadian soldiers take the weight off their feet for a trench-prepared snack*

It's similarly false to think that trenches were an innovation of the Great War. They had been in use at least two centuries before, in the Spanish Wars of Succession of the 18th century, and had also appeared in the American Civil War (1861-1865), the Second Anglo-Boer War (1899-1902) and the Russia-Japanese War of 1904-1905. But it's safe to say that trench warfare reached its apotheosis in World War I. Once the Race to the Sea had been run, both sides were dug in and there was no way round the lines of trenches that stretched from the North Sea to Switzerland.

There was a wide variation in the nature of the trenches between those two points. In the Somme valley, for example, the chalky soil was prone to crumbling after rain, so the trench walls had to be faced with timber, sandbags or whatever was available. In some places in France, trenches ran through towns and villages, across railway lines and rivers, through industrial sites and coalmines. The men whose job it was to dig in were forced to invent and improvise to meet the various challenges. In the muddy, low-lying lands of Flanders, it was not so much a case of digging in as building up: the men used sandbags and wood to manufacture their defences and parapets. Sometimes, as offensives were planned and executed in short periods of time, trenches would be little more than temporary affairs dug to a depth of perhaps 50 centimetres.

There was a fairly formalised pattern to trenches that were expected to shelter troops for an extended period, however. The front line would usually consist of a main fire trench facing the enemy, not always cut in a straight line but following the natural contours and features of the land. The lack of straight lines had another advantage: digging in sections, or bays, would limit damage to a particular section if a shell exploded in it; and if some of the enemy managed to infiltrate a bay, they might more easily be contained in that area.

Behind the fire trench was another line of excavations called the support line. Here could be found dugouts cut into the trench wall with enough room to shelter perhaps three or four men or accommodate a signalling point or

telephone position. Perhaps a platoon or company HQ could be found here.

To connect the areas at the rear to fire trenches and support lines, communication trenches would be dug. Along these lines would be ferried the equipment and supplies needed by the men at the front. And extending from the front line were further trenches known as saps, which probed beyond the protective tangles of barbed wire and ended in No Man's Land. These were manned by one or two soldiers who would be engaged in listening and observing.

Wherever it was possible, the floors of trenches would be covered with wooden duckboards. And lengths of wood had another purpose: they would be used to form a seat of sorts over the latrine. This would generally be as deep a hole as could be dug.

These, then, were the physical basics of trench life, which followed a fairly strict cycle. An Allied battalion would typically serve a period in the front line (some longer than others) that would be followed by a spell in support and a further period in the reserve lines. These stints would then be followed by a period of rest, often all too short and

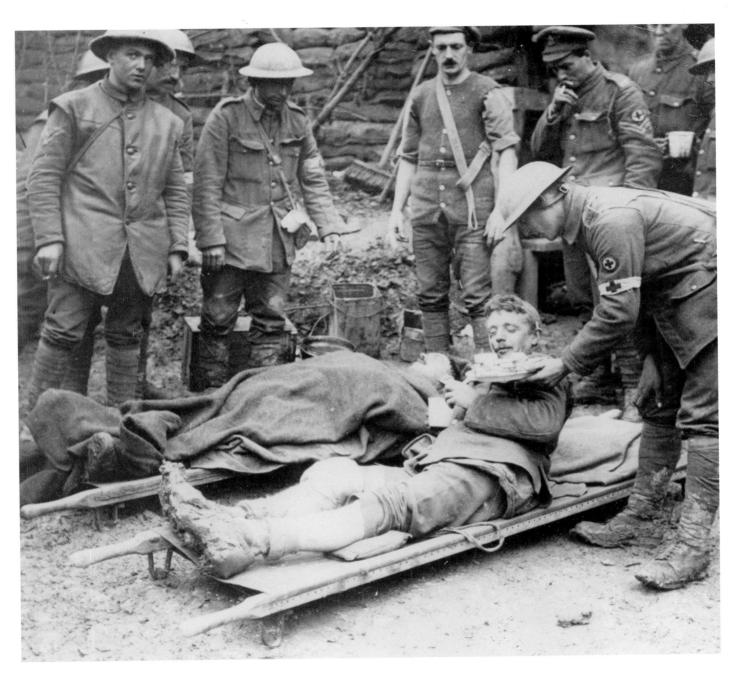

Right: *Bayonet fixed, a soldier keeps watch while his comrades catch some sleep*

sometimes interrupted by duties that would put the men back in the line of fire. And then the whole cycle would begin again.

Although practices varied widely, an infantryman might, during the course of a year on the Western Front, find himself passing 70 days in the front line and another 70 in support trenches. Perhaps 120 days would be spent in reserve — although the length of time would depend largely on where our infantryman was and what was happening around him — and around 70 days at rest. As for leave, when a soldier might expect to get away from the war altogether and perhaps see his home and loved ones, two weeks might be granted during a year.

Life in the trenches was a life of routine. Every morning, an hour before dawn, troops would be roused from wherever they had managed to bed down by the order to 'stand to'. Clambering stiffly to their feet, the troops would check their rifles were loaded, fix bayonets and climb up on the fire step — a step cut into the trench wall two or three feet above ground, enabling soldiers to peer towards the enemy lines. It was a fact of Great War life that attacks were usually mounted at dawn, despite the fact that both sides knew the enemy would be prepared to face an assault by the 'stand to' order.

It was another fact of life that stand to would be accompanied by another ritual – the morning hate. This was the opportunity to alleviate some of the early morning tension, and perhaps catch a dawn raid on the hop, by loosing off some rifle or machine gun rounds in the direction of the enemy lines.

Stand to might be followed by the issue of a rum ration, and then the men would start the important task of cleaning their rifles. Officers would then carry out rifle inspection before the equally important matter of breakfast was attended to. A remarkable aspect of the Great War was the observation by both sides, in some places, of an unofficial breakfast truce. As long as officers didn't stamp down on the practice, the men's fast could be broken in comparative peace and quiet.

The day would continue with inspection of the troops by a company or platoon commander and the assignment of chores by a non-commissioned officer. Perhaps duckboards on the trench floors needed repair; maybe trenches had to be drained; trench walls might be in need of repair before they collapsed; sandbags might need to be refilled; latrines might have to be dug. The NCOs were capable of dreaming up a million little jobs, some essential, some of less importance, to fill the troops' time.

Nevertheless, despite the NCOs' imaginations, boredom played a big part in the life of the men in the trenches. There couldn't be much movement until night fell, given the presence of snipers in the enemy lines, and the daylight hours between chores had to be filled somehow. This was the time for a few minutes of gratefully snatched sleep or for writing home. Otherwise, there would be long stretches of doing nothing in particular.

As night fell, the morning ritual of stand to would be repeated and then the men got busy. Some would be assigned to sentry duty of up to two hours on the fire step, but woe betide any man who let his fatigue get the better of him: the penalty for falling asleep on sentry duty was execution by firing squad.

Otherwise, soldiers might be told to fetch rations and water from the rear lines or undertake further maintenance

of the trenches. The hazardous job of barbed wire repair in No Man's Land might be on the agenda; men might be assigned to listening posts; others might simply be sent out on patrol beyond the front line. Sometimes a patrol might meet a similar group on a sortie from the enemy lines. Then the options were to fight hand to hand or simply get out of the way; to fire at your enemy in this situation would attract machine gun fire in a matter of seconds. The hours of

Above: *Precious sleep during the Battle of Thiepval Ridge, 1916*

darkness also provided an opportunity for men to be relieved of their front-line duty and replaced by reluctant troops making their way through the communications trenches weighed down by equipment.

To say that life was hazardous in the trenches is to state the obvious, but danger did not just come from enemy assaults or raids. In many locations there would be near-constant bombardment from the enemy artillery, and if a certain shell had your number on it … well, there was an end to trench life. Many a new boy on the front line also learned the hard way that snipers were ready at all times to punish those foolhardy enough to peer carelessly above the parapet.

Then there was the animal life, which prospered in the fetid atmosphere of the trenches. The most feared beasts were the rats that were simply everywhere in their millions, possessed of the temerity to scamper across a sleeping man's face. These animals seldom went hungry because of the ready availability of human corpses, and they could grow to the size of a cat. They spread disease and they contaminated food. Men tried in desperation, but without success, to diminish the rats' burgeoning populations, clubbing them, stamping on them, stabbing them with bayonets, shooting them.

There were other vermin to contend with. Lice were just as impossible to get rid of as rats. Even when infested clothing was washed and deloused, they left their eggs in the seams, waiting for a soldier's body heat to spur them to hatch. It was not until 1918 that lice were identified as the cause of another hazard – trench fever, an ailment that brought with it severe pain and high fever. Recovery took men away from the trenches for up to 12 weeks.

In wet, unsanitary trenches, the nasty fungal condition of trench foot was a constant threat. Affected feet could turn gangrenous, necessitating amputation. And then there was the ever-present irritant of nits – many men chose to shave their heads to deter the little beasts.

Finally, not least of the curses to affect trench inhabitants was the smell. The foul odour of unwashed bodies, rotting corpses, overflowing latrines, stagnant mud, cordite, poison gas and rotting sandbags could be guaranteed to provoke retching among first-time visitors to the trenches. Life in the trenches was no bed of roses.

Far Left: *British soldiers grab some food while a comrade keeps watch*

The World at War

While an entrenched, muddy and bloody war of attrition was taking place in France and Belgium, events to the east took a far different form. War on the Eastern Front, provoked by the Austro-Hungarian invasion of Serbia in July 1914, was a more fluid affair with much more toing and froing than in the West. This was a result of the vast geography of the front, which stretched from the Baltic Sea in the West to Minsk in the East and from St Petersburg in the North to the Black Sea in the South. This was a front of more than 1,600 kilometres and the density of troops defending it was far lower than on the Western Front, meaning it could be broken more easily. Trench warfare never really developed to any great extent in the East.

Tsar Nicholas II's Imperial Russian Army, once it had mobilised, represented a fearsome foe. Operating under the command of the Tsar's cousin Grand Duke Nicholas, it could call on 1.2 million men including 70 infantry and 24 cavalry divisions with a battery of almost 7,900 field guns, howitzers and heavy guns. The first action it saw came with the Russian invasion of East Prussia and the Austro-Hungarian province of Galicia – an action that suffered early defeat in the Battle of Tannenberg in August 1914. In this engagement the Russian forces were almost completely annihilated by the German Eighth Army. The Russians encountered more success

Right: *Australian camps on the slopes of Mount Scopus and the Mount of Olives during the Palestine Campaign*

as the year wore on, however, and by the end of 1914 it controlled almost all of Galicia.

The loss forced Germany to bolster its Austrian allies by committing more forces to the East in the form of its newly created Ninth Army. Fighting had moved into the centre of Russian Poland, where the Battle of the Vistula River in October and the Battle of Lódz in November and December – the latter fought in terrible winter conditions – provided little advancement for the Germans. The remainder of the winter saw the Austro-Hungarian and Russian armies engaging in the Carpathian Mountains, with defeats for both sides.

Boosting their forces in the East even further, and by now operating under a unified command, the Central Powers of Germany and Austria-Hungary launched the Gorlice-Tarnow Offensive in Galicia in May 1915. The Russians, suffering shortages of equipment, were on the retreat and had by the middle of the year been pushed out of Russian Poland. The

threat to the Central Powers' borders had been removed, but their advance stalled by the end of 1915.

The following year saw a reversal of fortunes as Russia, boosted by increases in industrial output and imports, went on the offensive. It claimed a resounding victory in the Brusilov Offensive of June 1916, aimed at the south-western front and resulting in the capture of hundreds of thousands of prisoners. But German reinforcements once again made a difference and the defeat of Russia's new ally Romania brought the Tsar's advance to a halt in September.

In 1917 there was another turning point: the Russian economy was under tremendous strain, and in February civil unrest in the cities, brought about by food shortages, escalated into the first of two revolutions in the country in that year. The Tsar abdicated amid increasing disaffection, and the last Russian initiative in the Great War proved to be the catastrophic Kerensky Offensive, in which Russia incurred 60,000 casualties,

Far Right:
German troops guard Italian prisoners taken during the 12th and final Battle of Isonzo, 1917

in Galicia in July. Lenin's Bolsheviks took power in November and endeavoured to end the war, but peace negotiations failed in February 1918.

Germany thereafter made massive inroads into Russian territory, meeting little resistance. With German troops within 150 kilometres of the capital Petrograd, the signing of the Treaty of Brest-Litovsk on March 3 sealed Russia's exit from the war and brought hostilities on the Eastern Front to an end.

Casualties had been enormous, particularly on the Russian side. As many as 2.2 million Russians were killed or reported missing, while 2.7 million were wounded and 3.3 million taken prisoner. In addition, there were 660,000 Romanian casualties. Among the Central Powers, a total of 7.4 million people were killed, missing, wounded or taken prisoner. And Germany and the Austro-Hungarian Empire were destined to lose all the land they had gained, and more, at the end of the war.

To the south, the Ottoman Empire, like its Austro-Hungarian ally, was fated to be deprived of its very existence. The empire entered the war following the signing of a secret Ottoman-German Alliance on 2 August 1914, and the Middle East subsequently saw conflict in five main campaigns: those of Sinai and Palestine, Mesopotamia, the Caucasus, Persia and Gallipoli. The campaigns' prime participants were on one side the Ottomans, with aid from the Central Powers, and on the other the British Empire with assistance from France and Russia.

It was Britain and many of its colonies that took on the Ottoman and German Empires in the Sinai and Palestine campaigns, which lasted from January 1915 until shortly before the end of the Great War. They began when a German-Ottoman force invaded Egypt's Sinai Peninsula and attacked the strategically important Suez Canal. During 1916 and early 1917 the peninsula was recaptured in an offensive from Australian, New Zealand and British forces, but that victory was followed by emphatic defeats in two battles for the town of Gaza in Palestine. Fortunes were reversed when British victory in the Third Battle of Gaza was followed by the capture of large territories including Jerusalem. Further success was to follow, and after the Egyptian Expeditionary Force had destroyed three Ottoman armies the

THE CONCISE HISTORY OF **WWI**

Ottomans agreed to end the conflict with the Armistice of Mudros in October 1918. It had lost the Sinai Peninsula, Palestine, Syria and Lebanon.

Mesopotamia, an ancient land through which run the Tigris and Euphrates rivers, had been part of the Ottoman Empire for centuries while never being completely under its control. The region held vitally important reserves of oil needed by Britain for its navy, and the latter decided early in the Great War that it needed to protect its interests by occupying the oilfields and pipeline near Basra.

The campaign that ensued involved mainly Indian and Australian troops, who succeeded in capturing Basra in November 1914 and then set out in pursuit of further prizes. Chief among these was Baghdad, the main city of Mesopotamia. In late 1915 the Poona Division advanced up-river only be forced to retreat to Kut-al-Amara as the year closed, and as 1916 dawned the city was surrounded and cut off. Attempts to relieve Kut were in vain and the garrison surrendered to Ottoman forces in April.

Taking charge of the British army in Mesopotamia, Major-General Stanley Maude introduced new thinking, with the result that the Ottomans suffered decisive defeats culminating in the capture of Baghdad in March 1917. British and Russian forces continued to close in, but no more decisive victories were attained. Losses on both sides totalled around 200,000.

The Caucasus Campaign saw conflict between Russia and the Ottoman Empire in a region where Europe meets Asia. The Ottomans' supreme commander, Enver Pasha, sought to recover Armenian territories lost to Russia in 1877-78, and went about it by launching an offensive in December 1914 with 100,000 troops. It was a poorly planned initiative. The mountainous terrain and the difficulties of winter warfare in such a region counted against Enver, who lost 86 per cent of his forces in the disastrous Battle of Sarikamish.

The Ottoman forces were driven out of the southern Caucasus in a series of Russian victories in 1915 and 1916, and plans were laid for a railway from Georgia to the conquered territories. The Tsar's abdication in 1917 put paid to those plans as the Russian army started to disintegrate. Its forces were replaced by those of Armenian volunteer and irregular units and conflict continued until the Armistice of Mudros. It took

Far Left:
Lancashire Fusiliers pack a boat before landing at Gallipoli, May 1915

Far Right:
*Portuguese troops
ready to embark
for Angola, 1915*

that same armistice to end the Persian Campaign, in which a number of engagements took place in northern Persian Azerbaijan and western Persia between the British and Russian Empires and the Ottoman Empire.

Ottoman victory was the result of one of the most infamous campaigns of the Great War, known throughout the world simply as Gallipoli. The plan, dreamed up by British First Lord of the Admiralty Winston Churchill, was for the Allies to open up a new front with which the Central Powers could not cope, and force a new passage through the Dardanelles, the narrow strait in north-western Turkey that connects the Aegean Sea to the Sea of Marmara. Creating another front would, Churchill believed, drain Germany of forces on the Western and Eastern Fronts as it came to the aid of its Ottoman allies, which he saw as the Central Powers' soft underbelly. The city of Constantinople could be taken, Turkey could be knocked out of the war and a route to Russia could be opened up. In the event, the campaign was based on flawed reasoning, was poorly planned and executed and led to one of the Allies' most disastrous defeats – and

Churchill's demotion.

On 19 February 1915, the Allies opened up a naval assault on Turkish positions in the Dardanelles and British and Anzac (Australian and New Zealand) troops were put on standby in Egypt. It went badly and the attack was abandoned after three battleships had been sunk and three others damaged. By the time Allied troops began to land on April 25, Ottoman preparations were complete: fortifications had been built and the defending forces had been multiplied sixfold.

Anzac forces, against formidable opposition, managed to win a bridgehead at 'Anzac Cove' on the Aegean side of the peninsula, while British forces attempted to land at five points around Cape Helles but succeeded in establishing footholds at just three. There the progress halted, and Ottoman reinforcements continued to arrive on the peninsula. Back in London, Churchill was at loggerheads with Lord Fisher, the First Sea Lord, who resigned when his demand that the operation be discontinued was over-ruled. The Liberal government was replaced by a coalition and Churchill was relieved of his post.

The stalemate dragged on into the summer as Allied troops suffered

in scorching heat and disease-ridden conditions. In July the British reinforced the bridgehead at Anzac Cove and the following month attempted to seize the Sari Bair heights by landing troops at Suvla Bay, to the north. In the face of Ottoman counter-attacks, the initiative failed within days.

In late 1915 Britain decided to end the campaign and the troops were evacuated by the end of January 1916. The Allies had suffered 252,000 casualties, the Ottoman Empire a similar number and nothing much had been achieved, but there were other consequences of the Gallipoli campaign. British Prime Minister Herbert Asquith was soon replaced by David Lloyd George; an

Ottoman commander, Mustafa Kemal Atatürk, went on to lead the Turkish bid for independence and found the Republic of Turkey; and the Australian and New Zealand troops' sacrifice is marked each year on Anzac Day, April 25. Seldom has a single, relatively small-scale military campaign had such far-reaching consequences.

Although it was a member of the Triple Alliance with Germany and Austria-Hungary, Italy did not declare war in 1914. Its long-standing rivalry with Austria-Hungary lingered, and it was keen to claim territories in the Austrian Littoral, Cisalpine Tyrol and Dalmatia that it had lost in the previous century. Diplomatic efforts in the early part of the war focused on persuading Italy to co-operate with the Allies, and on 26 April 1915 the two sides signed the Treaty of London, which renounced Italy's ties with the Triple Alliance. Less than a month later, Italy declared war on Austria-Hungary.

The first step was an offensive designed to capture the town of Gorizia on the Isonzo river and highlands on the Kras plateau and in the western Julian March. Success would enable Italy to advance towards Trieste and Ljubljana. Although outnumbering the Austro-Hungarian enemy by three to one, the Italians were hampered by their occupation of lower ground, poor training and low morale, and the attempt foundered. Further assaults later in the year also failed, as did a 1916 Austro-Hungarian counter-offensive aimed at breaking through to the plain of the River Po.

Battles for the Isonzo continued throughout 1916. The sixth in the series, launched by the Italians in August, resulted in the taking of Gorizia at the foot of the Julian Alps and helped to bolster morale, but in general the unremitting warfare achieved little beyond the exhaustion of both armies. Much more was demanded of Italian troops than of the counterparts in the trenches of the Western Front: offensives were being launched every three months and the troops were subjected to exceptionally harsh discipline and punishments. In addition, shells fired in the rocky terrain of the campaign were around 70 per cent more deadly than those expended in the softer ground of France and Belgium. And there were other hazards: on 13 December 1916, 10,000 troops met their deaths in avalanches in the Dolomite mountains. Small wonder that Italian morale plummeted.

Pushed back to near Venice in October 1917, the Italians received the aid of British and French troops, plus vital materials, the following month. Then, in 1918, came the withdrawal of German troops to boost their spring offensive on the Western Front, but the Austro-Hungarians were determined to finish the campaign with a two-pronged offensive in the Battle of the Piave River. It was repulsed, but to the disappointment of the Allies, Italy failed to follow up its success.

By October 1918, however, Italy was in a position to launch an offensive, and it did so with an attack targeting Vittorio Veneto, across the Piave. Breaking through, the Italian army rushed in reinforcements and wiped out the Austrian defences. On November 3, 300,000 Austro-Hungarian troops surrendered in a move that signalled the end of the empire's army as an effective fighting force. More importantly, it heralded the dissolution of the empire, with declarations of independence being made in Budapest, Prague and Zagreb.

An armistice, signed on November 3 in Padua brought the Italian campaign to an end. Both sides had endured enormous losses: 651,000 killed and nearly a million wounded on the Allied side; 404,000 killed and 1.2 million wounded for the Central Powers.

The continent of Africa could not escape the deadly attentions of World War I. German colonies, mostly lightly defended, were subject

to campaigns by armies of the British Empire, France, Belgium and Portugal, and by the end of the war Germany's empire outside Europe had been dismantled, with the victors dividing the spoils between them.

German colonial troops in the West African country of Togoland (nowadays Togo and the Volta region of Ghana) surrendered to British and French forces very early in the war, but in Kamerun (modern-day Cameroon) the fight

Above:
Russian forces at the Battle of Sarikamish during the Caucasus campaign, 1915

continued until 1916, after many soldiers had escaped into the neutral territory of Spanish Guinea.

In their attempt to take German South-West Africa (known today as Namibia), the British initially committed the error of arming their former enemies the Boers of South Africa, and paid the price when 12,000 Boers rebelled. Once the rebels had been beaten, Boer General Jan Smuts advanced on the capital, Windhoek, and succeeded in capturing it in May 1915. South Africa was to be the effective ruler of South-West Africa for the next 75 years.

German and Portuguese forces clashed on the border between South-West Africa and Angola in March 1915. Despite early success, the Germans surrendered in July.

undefeated, for four years. By 1916 the British had tired of the hit–and–run tactics and handed command to Smuts, who proceeded to achieve moderate success. It was only after being informed of the German capitulation in Europe, in November 1918, that Lettow-Vorbeck agreed first to a ceasefire and then to surrender. While he had had little influence on the overall outcome of the Great War, he returned to Germany a national hero.

It was a different story in East Africa, where the German colony comprised the modern-day states of Tanzania, Burundi and Rwanda. Here, in a heroic guerrilla campaign led by the German General Paul von Lettow-Vorbeck, a force of no more than 14,000 (including 11,000 Africans) held the combined, 300,000-strong armies of Britain, Belgium and Portugal at bay,

The Allies faced a task in China and the Pacific Ocean that was similar to the one encountered in Africa: the conquest of German and Austrian colonial possessions. Most of these fell without blood being spilled, but naval warfare was widespread: all of the world's colonial powers, including Germany, had naval presences in the Indian or Pacific Oceans.

The Siege of Tsingtao of 1914, probably the most significant engagement of the Asian theatre, was the first encounter between Japanese and German forces and also saw the first joint Anglo-Japanese operation of the war. The eastern Chinese city of Tsingtao, nowadays known as Qingdao,

was the base of the German Navy's East Asia Squadron, which operated in support of the power's territories in the region and was garrisoned by 4,000 troops. On August 15, Japan issued an ultimatum demanding that Germany withdraw its warships from Chinese and Japanese waters and cede control of Tsingtao to Japan. Three days later the ultimatum expired and Japan declared war.

Bombardment of the port began on September 2. The Japanese General Mitsuomi Kamio, who had at his disposal 23,000 men supported by 142 guns, employed siege tactics that drew

admiration from the watching British (suspicious of Japanese motives, Britain had sent 1,500 troops to keep an eye on proceedings). Kamio favoured night raids and avoided the kind of bloody frontal assault that was to become common thousands of miles away on the Western Front. The German garrison was outnumbered by six to one yet managed to hold out for over two months before surrendering on November 7 and handing over the port three days later. Germany had lost two ships, 727 men killed and 1,335 wounded. When defeat seemed certain, the German Empire had scuttled its squadron.

Air and Sea

Far Right: *A Zeppelin fails to cause panic as it passes over a peaceful London street*

The years of the Great War witnessed huge changes in the ways in which man went about the grim business of warfare, as we have seen in the preceding chapters. But it was not just on land that transformations were wrought; while the navies of the great powers clashed on the oceans, the way was being opened up to a future in which supremacy in the air was crucial for success in war.

The comparatively recent invention of powered aircraft – Wilbur and Orville Wright had made their first sustained flight in a heavier-than-air, powered aeroplane in 1903 – played a major role in World War I. Planes began to be used by the world's military powers just as the war was breaking out and were initially used mainly for reconnaissance, but advancement was rapid as the years wore on. Learning from experience, engineers and manufacturers were soon developing increasingly sophisticated fighter, bomber and ground–attack aircraft.

At first, however, many senior military men were sceptical of the warfare potential of fixed-wing aircraft. Zeppelin airships were often seen as the ideal for reconnaissance and bombing missions, although the bombardment of London by German Zeppelin crews was often more valuable in psychological rather than military terms. In August 1914 the German army possessed about

THE CONCISE HISTORY OF **WWI**

230 fixed-wing aircraft, but only around 180 were in a usable state. Britain was a late starter in aeronautical terms and relied largely on the French, especially for the manufacture of engines. Three squadrons of about 30 aircraft were available to the Royal Flying Corps (which had been founded in 1912), while the US's minimal contribution to the air war could safely be discounted.

Reconnaissance from the air played a pivotal role in the early months of the war in western Europe; an outstanding example of its usefulness came when the lives of 100,000 soldiers were saved thanks to a British withdrawal towards Mons in Belgium as a result of aerial snooping on German movements. Little thought was given to the idea of aerial combat, and there are even stories of rival reconnaissance crews exchanging friendly greetings as they passed.

Aircraft in 1914 could carry only small bomb loads, yet the devastation of today's bombing warfare can be dated back to raids such as the one carried out by the Royal Navy's air arm on German airship bases late in that year. Meanwhile, previously friendly reconnaissance crews were progressing to throwing grenades and even grappling hooks at each other's machines, and the first aircraft brought down by another was an Austrian plane rammed by a Russian pilot in September 1914. Soon, pilots were firing inaccurate hand-held guns at each other, and then, in October 1914, French pilot Louis Quenault launched a machine-gun attack on a German aircraft.

Once the problem of mounting machine guns whose rounds did not smash the plane's propeller blades – the British Vickers FB5 and the French Morane-Saulnier L were early examples of purpose-designed fighters – the air war was truly under way and the era of the air ace was born. In July 1915, Germany overtook the Allies in introducing the Fokker E I monoplane, initiating an era known as the Fokker Scourge when the Central Powers achieved air superiority with pilots including Max Immelmann (the Eagle of Lille, credited with 15 aerial victories) among the earliest aces.

The Allies hit back with new machines including the British FE2b and DH2 and the French Nieuport 11, and won back air superiority in time for the Battle of the Somme in 1916. Fighters were now being used to destroy observation balloons, attack

Far Left: *A German Fokker D VII fighter in aerobatic action*

ground targets and defend airspace against bombers. In late 1915 came the first flight of the Junkers J1 monoplane, an all-metal aircraft that showed the way forward for aviation technology. Despite the technical advances and new aircraft taking to the air, fighter pilots were being sent into battle with precious little flying time under their belts. Yet in the Somme pilots on both sides were undertaking the dangerous task of trench strafing – a challenge that became even more perilous as the war dragged on and defence techniques developed.

In 1916, the German High Command initiated the organisation of specialist bomber and fighter squadrons and by the beginning of the following year had achieved superiority once again, aided by aircraft such as the Fokker D I, D II and D III and the Albatros D I. The Allies, despite the introduction of fighters such as the Sopwith Pup and Triplane and SPAD SVII, endured Bloody April in 1917 when the RFC suffered particularly heavy losses. Back swung the pendulum, however, when the British Sopwith Camel, among other machines, became available in the latter part of the year.

During the Germans' Spring Offensive of 1918, the Allies' air superiority was maintained at a heavy price. Casualties reached the highest level since Bloody April as the sheer weight of numbers of machines and

pilots available allowed the Allies to hold the upper hand. In this they were helped by the introduction of American squadrons flying European-designed aircraft. By the end of the war, American Brigadier-General Billy Mitchell was

able to declare with confidence: 'The day has passed when armies on the ground or navies on the sea can be the arbiter of a nation's destiny in war. The main power of the defence and the power of initiative against an enemy has

THE CONCISE HISTORY OF **WWI**

Above: *12in guns on HMS Dreadnought, part of the British battleship's formidable battery*

passed to the air.'

Just as the growing importance of air-based warfare had grown, so too had the fame surrounding the men who flew the machines. Ace fighter pilots came to be regarded as folk heroes, with legends growing up around them similar to those that surrounded medieval knights. And of all the air aces, no one had a greater reputation than Manfred von Richthofen. With a 'score' of 80 combat victories, the Red Baron was a flamboyant flyer whose brightly painted Fokker DR-1 triplane was instantly recognisable – as were his skills. Behind him in the table of air victories were the

Above: *HMS Bellerophon, a dreadnought battleship that operated in the British Fourth Battle Squadron*

French René Fonck, with a tally of 75, and the Canadian William Bishop with 72. Men like these helped to establish the strategic importance of aerial warfare of which Mitchell spoke.

While there was less rapid technological development among the major powers' navies during World War I than in the air, hostilities had been preceded by a hectic arms race that saw Germany competing with Britain to build 'dreadnought' battleships and challenge the latter's unquestioned supremacy on the seas. When the first of the type, the Royal

Navy's *HMS Dreadnought*, was launched in 1906 she made a huge impact on the watching nations. They were impressed by her 'all-big-gun' armament scheme – featuring an unprecedented number of large calibre guns – and her revolutionary steam turbine propulsion, and dreadnought races started up throughout the world. The naval arms race was an important contributor to the

heightening tensions that led to the war.

Regardless of the number of dreadnoughts each side possessed, naval warfare during the Great War mainly consisted of attempts by the Allied Powers to blockade the Central Powers and the latter's bid to blockade Britain and France, largely using their submarine fleet. Encounters took place mainly around the British Isles and in

Germany. The RN's Harwich Force consisted of two light cruisers and two flotillas of 31 destroyers, with the First Battle Cruiser Squadron – two battleships and three battle cruisers – acting as cover. Having sunk two German torpedo boats, the British found themselves outgunned and called for assistance, which was duly provided by the covering squadron, under the command of Vice-Admiral David Beatty. By the time the Germans retreated they had lost seven cruisers and 1,200 men. Beatty's reputation was enhanced and the action was influential in his promotion to the position of Commander-in-Chief of the Grand Fleet later in the war.

The Battle of Coronel off the coast of Chile resulted from a search by Admiral Sir Christopher Cradock's West Indies Squadron for a German commerce-raiding squadron operating under Admiral Maximilian von Spee in the Pacific. Cradock's forces were no match, however, for Spee's five-vessel force, which included the armoured cruisers *Scharnhorst* and *Gneisenau* and three light cruisers. Battle commenced unexpectedly early on 1 November 1914 and resulted in the outgunned

the Atlantic Ocean, although the Baltic Sea, Black Sea and the Indian and Pacific Oceans also saw major action. A number of significant battles occupy prominent positions in the annals of naval warfare.

The first of these took place on 28 August 1914, when the Battle of Heligoland Bight saw the Royal Navy attacking shipping located close to a naval base on the coast of north-west

Right: *British sailors watch the sinking of SMS Mainz during the Battle of Heligoland Bight, 1914. The British rescued 348 men from the light cruiser before she sank*

Cradock losing his flagship *Good Hope*, the armoured cruiser *Monmouth*, all hands and his own life.

When news of the humiliating defeat reached Britain, the Admiralty started to assemble a vast force under Admiral Sir Frederick Sturdee to exact revenge on Spee. The result was the Battle of the Falkland Islands, which began on December 8. Spee had sailed for the islands with the aim of raiding their British radio station and coaling depot. Little did he know that the powerful British cruisers *Invincible* and *Inflexible* were already at Port Stanley, accompanied by six other cruisers. Spee, mistaking the British shipping for Japanese, began his attack but soon realised his error and made for the open sea, pursued by the British. During the ensuing battle four German cruisers including the flagship *Scharnhorst* were sunk and 2,200 sailors were either killed or drowned. The battle brought the German raids on commerce to an end and reversed the setback to British morale that had been inflicted at Coronel.

Sea battles continued throughout 1915, and they included the Battle of Dogger Bank in the North Sea on January 24, which resulted in British

victory. But the most significant of them all, the Battle of Jutland, opened on 31 May 1916. It ended with both Britain and Germany claiming victory.

The Commander of the German High Seas Fleet, Reinhardt Scheer, was intent on making a sortie against the British coast confident that his plans were unknown to the main British battle fleet based at Scapa Flow in the North of Scotland. His confidence was misplaced as Admiral Sir John Jellicoe, able to read his messages, knew exactly what he was about. Engaged in chasing battle cruisers under Admiral Beatty, Scheer suddenly found his vessels under bombardment from Jellicoe's fleet and was forced to order a retreat. Then Scheer made the mistake of turning back, perhaps hoping to pass behind Jellicoe and escape into the Baltic, and found his fleet passing in front of the British. Ten minutes of gunfire inflicted 27 heavy hits while the British suffered just two, and Scheer again ordered a retreat. There followed a night of intense fighting in which Germany lost one battle cruiser, one pre-dreadnought battleship, four light cruisers and five destroyers, while the British suffered to the tune of three battle cruisers, four armoured cruisers and eight destroyers. The result of the battle was effectively a draw, but Jutland, the last of the great sea battles, did end the threat of the High Seas Fleet and leave control of the North Sea with the Royal Navy.

Britain subsequently mounted North Sea operations including the Zeebrugge Raid on 23 April 1918, which was designed to neutralise the Belgian port by sinking older British ships in the port's canal entrance to prevent German vessels – including dangerous submarines – from leaving. The operation did not go as planned. Two hundred British sailors were killed and 300 wounded and the canal was blocked for only a few days, but the raid was promoted by Allied propaganda as a significant victory and eight Victoria Crosses were awarded.

Despite the failure of Zeebrugge, Britain maintained its superiority over Germany on the oceans, with the North Sea theatre proving the crucial area of operations. The Allied blockade on commerce through the North Sea eventually led to the starvation of Germany's industry and people, which was a major influence on its decision to seek the Armistice of November 1918.

Far Left: *The single-seater Sopwith Camel, a superb fighter credited with shooting down 1,294 enemy aircraft*

Peace at What Cost?

The guns fell silent one by one, Kaiser Wilhelm II abdicated on 9 November 1918 and finally, at 5.10am on November 11, the Armistice with Germany was signed. When it came into effect at 11am that day and hostilities ceased, it meant that the end of the Great War had come at the 11th hour of the 11th day of the 11th month. It is an hour that will be remembered as long as the human race exists.

Even before the Armistice with Germany, the Central Powers had been in utter disarray. The Austro-Hungarian Empire was no more: in late October the Serbs, Croats and Slovenes had announced the establishment of a new Slavic state to be called Yugoslavia, and Hungary had declared its independence; the Austrian armistice was signed on November 3, and Austria-Hungary ceased to exist. The Ottoman Empire had signed peace terms on October 30, and most of its territories were to be redistributed and eventually reorganised into independent countries.

In Germany, the situation was chaotic. There had been fears before the war's end of a Bolshevik-style workers' revolution, and upon the Kaiser's abdication left-wing groups proclaimed the establishment of both a Soviet Republic and a Socialist Republic. Neither would become reality.

But if the bloodshed had stopped on the battlefield, the manoeuvring off it had barely begun. There was a treaty to be

drafted and signed and it was to be another seven months before arrangements for a lasting peace between all the powers had been settled. The diplomatic jostling at the end of the war proved just as tortuous as it had before the outbreak of hostilities.

American President Woodrow Wilson had been the most prominent world leader in the months leading up to the end of the war, proclaiming his ideal outcomes for the international arena in a speech that became known as the Fourteen Points. Among Wilson's desires were the prohibition of secret treaties, the right of a country's people to self-determination and international co-operation. Now he wanted his Fourteen Points to form the basis of the treaties that would mark the end of the war.

At the Paris Peace Conference that convened on 19 January 1919, Wilson and his entourage rubbed shoulders with politicians and diplomats from 32 countries. Among them were his fellows in the 'Big Four': Prime Minister David Lloyd George of Great Britain, French Prime Minister Georges Clemenceau and Vittorio Orlando, the Italian Premier. Germany and Russia were not invited, but multitudes of monarchs, political leaders and their advisers, journalists and lobbyists were there, each straining to be heard above the hubbub and stressing the importance of his cause. For six months Paris formed the centre of a kind of world government, reshaping the map of Europe, dividing up the Central Powers' colonies in Africa, Asia and the Pacific and setting up the League of Nations, an international organisation designed to prevent wars through collective security and disarmament. The League of Nations, lacking the United States as a member, was weakened from the start and was destined not to last beyond the end of World War II.

The Treaty of Versailles, signed on June 28 – exactly five years after the assassination of Franz Ferdinand – was the most important of the peace treaties that came out of the Paris conference, for it dealt with Germany. Crucially, one of its provisions (the so-called War Guilt Clause) required Germany to accept its responsibility, and that of its allies, for all the loss and damage suffered during the war. Germany would also be obliged to disarm, concede extensive territories and pay enormous sums by way of reparation to member countries of the Allies. Two years after the Treaty, the cost of the reparations was put at £6.6

Far Left: *Leaders of the Big Four at the 1919 Paris Peace Conference, from left British Prime Minister David Lloyd George, Italian Prime Minister Vittorio Orlando, French Prime Minister Georges Clemenceau and US President Woodrow Wilson*

billion, a sum that would work out today at around £284 billion. Some of the Entente's leaders, notably France, judged the reparations to be just; others felt they were over-harsh. They would, in any case, be abolished in 1932.

The Treaty, in truth, represented a compromise with which no party was truly satisfied – no surprise, given the sheer mass of conflicting claims that had been presented at Paris. Germany was left humiliated, and neither pacified nor conciliated. Among the territories it lost were Alsace-Lorraine and much of present-day Poland. It was allowed to keep the border region of the Rhineland while being forbidden to develop it militarily. And most harshly in the eyes of the German leaders and many millions of its people, it was forced to acknowledge and accept full responsibility for the war and all that had occurred during it. Not only was this acknowledgment impossible for many Germans to accept, it was also based on a falsehood.

The Great War had begun with an opportunistic assassination and diplomatic manoeuvring. After four years of unimaginable hardship, senseless slaughter, stupidity, duplicity and destruction, the face of war had been changed for ever and tens of millions of combatants and civilians lay dead. Entire countries lay in ruins, as did their economies and those of other nations. Thanks to the existence of the European powers' empires – some of which no longer existed – men from every corner of the globe had been drawn into the conflict, many with little idea of what they were fighting for.

After most previous European wars, the two sides had shaken hands, accepted their losses or gains and resumed their lives. This was not possible after the Great War. Germany, in political chaos and economic meltdown, was vulnerable to the urgings of extremist politicians of both left and right wings. The rabble-rousers ranted that the Fatherland had been stabbed in the back by its leaders and foreign powers, which had connived to impoverish and emasculate a proud nation.

The Treaty of Versailles had in fact created the precise conditions that would, within 20 years, give rise to another terrible global conflict. Among those serving near the front line of the Western Front had been a young soldier who was wounded at the Battle of the Somme and was awarded the Iron Cross, First Class for bravery. His name was Adolf Hitler.

Right: *Adolf Hitler (left) with comrades at the Battle of the Somme, 1916*

ALSO AVAILABLE IN THE LITTLE BOOK SERIES

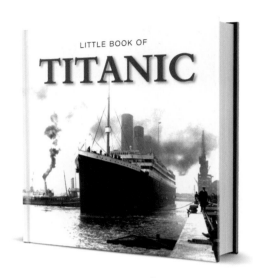

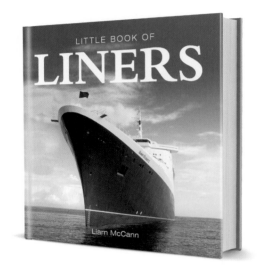

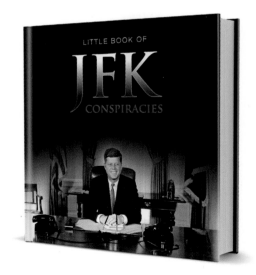

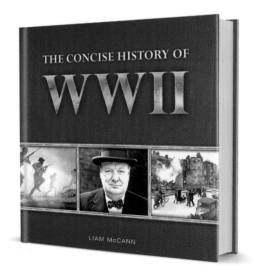

ALSO AVAILABLE IN THE LITTLE BOOK SERIES

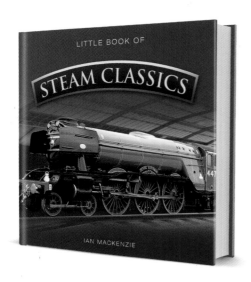

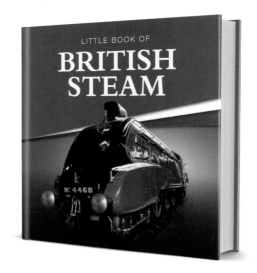

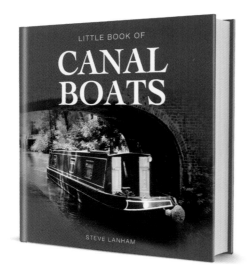

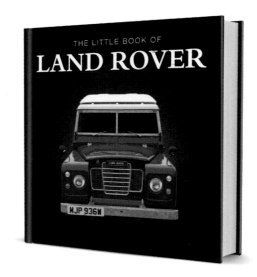

The pictures in this book were provided courtesy of the following:

WIKIMEDIA COMMONS

Design & Artwork: SCOTT GIARNESE

Published by: DEMAND MEDIA LIMITED & G2 ENTERTAINMENT LIMITED

Publishers: JASON FENWICK & JULES GAMMOND

Written by: PAT MORGAN